Cracking English Grammar in KS2

100+ Creative Games and Writing Activities

Brilliant
PUBLICATIONS

David Horner

Publisher's Information

We hope you and your pupils enjoy using the ideas in this book. Brilliant Publications publishes many other books to help primary school teachers. To find out more details on all of our titles, including those listed below, please go to our website: www.brilliantpublications.co.uk.

Also written by David Horner
  Cracking Creative Writing

Books in the Developing Reading Comprehension Skills series:
  Classic Poetry Years 3-4
  Classic Poetry Years 5-6
  Classic Children's Literature Years 3-4
  Classic Children's Literature Years 5-6
  Contemporary Children's Literature Years 3-4
  Contemporary Children's Literature Years 5-6
  Non-fiction Years 3-4
  Non-fiction Years 5-6

Brilliant Activities for Reading Comprehension series
Getting to Grips with English Grammar series
Brilliant Activities for Creative Writing series
Brilliant Activities for Grammar and Punctuation series
Boost Creative Writing series
Daily Sentence Structures

Published by Brilliant Publications Limited
Unit 10
Sparrow Hall Farm
Edlesborough
Dunstable
Bedfordshire
LU6 2ES, UK

www.brilliantpublications.co.uk

The name Brilliant Publications and the logo are registered trademarks.

Written by David Horner

© Brilliant Publications Limited 2021

Printed ISBN: 978-0-85747-848-1
ePDF ISBN: 978-0-85747-850-4
First printed in 2022

Contents

Contents

Cracking English Grammar in KS2 by David Horner

Contents

"For I am a Bear of Very Little Brain, and long words Bother me." A. A. Milne (1882–1956), *The World of Winnie-the-Pooh.*

And there do seem to be lots of long words in educational matters these days. I'll warn you now that several of them are crammed between the covers of this book, the focus of which is grammar, punctuation and spelling, as set out in the current English curriculum. Given the large (you might say overwhelming) quantity of material and issues in the Orders, my sole purpose in writing this book was to turn the terminology of NC SPaG into accessible activities – and creative fun!

You will recall that Winnie-the-Pooh makes his self-deprecating remark after Owl has been sounding off on the issue of 'customary procedure'. Winnie has never heard this phrase before, and so innocently asks Owl to explain the meaning of 'Crustimoney Proseedcake'. We've all known circumstances like that, in meetings with doctors, car mechanics, bank managers, plumbers – I'm certain you can name your own – where their expertise, clothed in long words, reduces us to believing we too are 'of Very Little Brain'.

It was not the long words themselves that cause the trouble. My experience working as a visiting writer in primary schools over many years showed me that young children actually liked them! From the names of exotic dinosaurs to the latest Premier League import, they relished their ability to show off their (frequently superior) knowledge to my own. No, the problem with long words is when they remain just that – words we can't make sense of because we can't attach them to something we already know and therefore add them meaningfully to our own vocabulary and understanding.

All of which brings me inevitably to literacy on Planet SPaG, specifically in Time-Zone KS2, where this issue of long words becomes most acute. The insistence that grammatical concepts and categories 'should be taught explicitly' makes it inevitable. However, and curiously, there is very little said about what children might actually do with all this learning, what they might actually go on and write. The Guidance calls this aspect 'composition' but mentions little beyond 'narrative' and 'non-narrative' material.

The belief seems to be that, once children have an explicit knowledge of grammar, they will inevitably be better writers all round. Well maybe, but I decided to be explicit myself and *Cracking English Grammar in KS2* is the result. In brief, I have taken each individual item of the KS2 SPaG agenda and designed a creative writing activity around it. I've written the 100+ activities with a fixed focus and precise structure, so children can readily explore and engage with both terminology and concept; they can see what the living language does and most importantly what they can do with the language, their language after all! We grown-ups take work seriously; children take play very seriously. So, I very much wanted these activities to be both purposeful and playful.

Introduction

I'm not at all against children having an amount of meta-language (language for describing language). It could be frustrating at times in the past, not to be able to discuss even basic terms such as adjective or verb tense. However, terminology is useful only if the understanding of it is shared and it's not just a dispiriting sequence of those long words. The English Guidance does hint at a need for marrying the terminology and actual writing by asking that children 'should be taught to use the elements of spelling, grammar, punctuation and 'language about language' listed… to provide a structure on which (teachers) can construct exciting lessons'. Well, I'll leave you to decide about exciting or otherwise, but that invitation might be where this book can make its contribution.

As with my previous book, *Cracking Creative Writing*, I've written directly to the young writer, who might be working alone, with a partner or as a group member. This doesn't mean, of course, that teachers can't take particular activities and use them for teaching to a whole or part of a class. My rule throughout has been that each concept, term and activity should be simply explained and take no more than an hour to complete. I've tried to keep matters concentrated but light in tone, focussing on those individual SPaG items in turn. Thus, young writers who play these games get to use structures, patterns and concepts in some directly and precisely related writing. The purpose throughout has been that children develop their linguistic understanding, competence and confidence through some immediate, enjoyable and hopefully memorable usage.

Because any teacher using this book will want to access an area of concern quickly, there is an index of grammatical terms and concepts on page 147. In the interests of honesty, I will admit that the book has nothing to offer on paragraphing and (sub)headings. I tried, but in the end felt these were best dealt with in relation to writing, in say, a science or a research topic. Sorry!

Many of the activities introduce different forms of poetry. Most children will be familiar with a haiku, but how many have had the chance to write a hexastich or a quinzaine? The index of poetic forms, on page 146, will help you find the activities to teach each of these forms easily.

Finally, a big thank you is due to those youngsters, not in school as I wrote, who helped me so much with trying and trialling some of these materials. It is to them this book is deservedly dedicated. It seems there is a term for those who suffer from a fear of long words; inevitably, it's a very long word itself – *hippopotomonstrosesquippedaliophobia* – but I know it's a word they will all savour, and a condition they'll never suffer from.

Snow had fallen in the night and the park was busy.

I made a snowball.

People were building snowmen or they were riding on sledges.

I hurled the snowball into the cold air.

The park was white all over but the trees were bare and black.

The snowball was coming down.

The roads around the park were icy so the traffic moved very slowly and carefully.

The snowball crashed onto this lady's back.

Gavin

Simple and Compound Sentences

There you have it – a whole story in just eight sentences! Look at it again and you will see that it is made of some long sentences and some short sentences. These sentences have names: the short ones are called **simple sentences** and the long ones are called **compound sentences**.

A **simple sentence** is usually just one **short clause** with one **main verb**. In Gavin's story his verbs are: *made*, *hurled*, *was coming* and *crashed*. Short, simple sentences keep the story moving.

A **compound sentence** is made out of two **simple sentences**, joined together by a tiny word with a big name – a **coordinating conjunction**. Gavin uses *and*, *or*, *but* and *so*. Each half of

---

          Cracking English Grammar in KS2 by David Horner

the compound sentence can make a simple sentence on its own. Longer sentences slow us down as we read, let us see a whole scene – and make us wait for what will happen next!

Now it's your turn

✳ Choose a scene for your story – and one main character. Gavin chose a snowy park and himself. Here are some suggestions for you to think about:

- trying to catch a ball at rounders or cricket
- a wasp in the kitchen
- a visit to the dentist
- a puppy's first walk
- taking a penalty kick
- a fairground ride

✳ Remember, you need four **simple sentences** for the story's action and four **compound sentences** to describe the scene.

✳ It might help you to write the sequence of your four simple sentences first. Write them as double-spaced lines, so then you can go back and write your compound sentences in the gaps between these lines.

Hint 1: Like Gavin, see if you can use a different conjunction in each of your compound sentences.

Hint 2: Gavin wrote his story in the past tense. You can do the same or use the present tense instead.

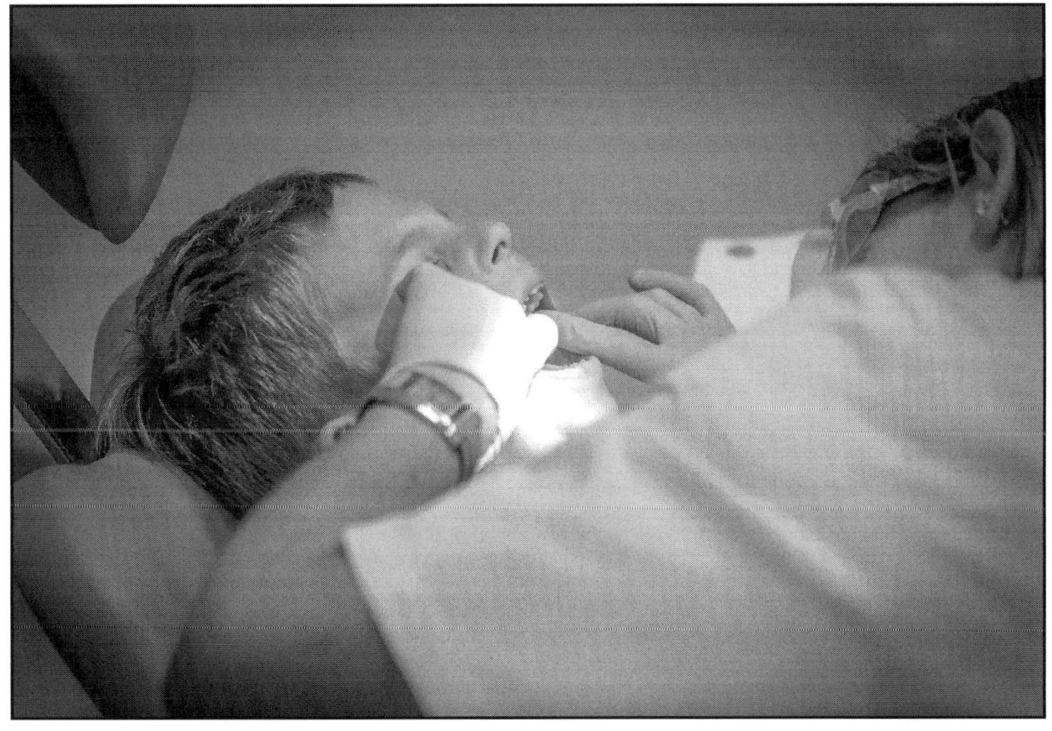

When the engines stop, everything falls silent.

    She goes to the doorway.

Silver steps go down, once the door is fully open.

    She walks out calmly.

There is a red landscape wherever she looks.

    She reaches the last step.

As soon as the signal comes, she steps down.

    She is the first woman on Mars.

Mia

Clauses and Sentences

Mia has made that story out of just eight sentences. Look again and you will see that she has written four short sentences and four longer ones. The short ones are called **simple sentences** and the longer ones are **complex sentences**.

A **simple sentence** has just one **main verb**. Mia used *goes*, *walks*, *reaches* and *is*.

A **complex sentence** is made of **two clauses**, each one with a **main verb**. For example, *stop/ falls* and *go/is*. Check to find the main verbs in the last two complex sentences.

A **complex sentence** has a **main clause** and a **subordinate clause**. The main clause can be a sentence on its own, like 'everything falls silent', but the subordinate clause doesn't make complete sense by itself. So, when Mia starts, 'When the engines stop', you know you need more. The two clauses are joined together by a subordinating conjunction; in Mia's story they are: *when*, *once*, *wherever*, and *as soon as*. Here are some more:

in spite of	owing to	before	by the time	meanwhile	although
even though	because of	now that	as long as	whenever	

Now it's your turn

✳ Like Mia, you need one character and one scene. Here are some more scenes for you

- Crossing a desert
- Winning a medal in the Olympics
- Getting lost in a forest
- Going up to receive the FA Cup
- Entering a spooky castle
- Appearing on stage

✳ Choose one of these or an idea of your own. Use the four simple sentences to say what your character does and the four complex sentences for your scene-setting and mood-building.

✳ You might start by writing your four simple sentences on double-spaced lines, leaving the spaces in between to add the complex sentences after.

✳ Try to use four different subordinating conjunctions in your work and mix the order of the clauses in different sentences.

Hint: Mia writes her story in the present tense. You can do the same, or use the past tense, even the future tense instead.

Vanishing Tricks

Vowels

Take a look the text below. It's called **Vnng**:

> ### Vnng
>
> Th dy s pst, th sn s st, nd th wht strs r n th sky; whl th lng grss wth dw s wt, nd thrgh th r th bts nw fly.

Can you work out some of the words? It would be much easier to read if all the **vowels** hadn't vanished! It shows how important vowels are. There are only five of them, but they do so much work: they appear in almost every word in the English language and they have to make 20 different sounds for us.

All those words make a four-line verse to a poem called 'Evening'. The poem has six verses all together, made entirely of one-syllable words. Clever!

Lines 1 and 3 and lines 2 and 4 rhyme. Can you spot the line breaks? Have a go at writing the verse out with all its vowels and in four rhymed lines. Try not to look but it is printed at the foot of this page for you to check. The poem was written by Thomas Miller, a nineteenth century writer born in Lincolnshire, who left school aged just nine years.

Now it's your turn

This is a good game to work on with a partner. It's even better if you can get another pair to compete against!

✳ The first thing you have to do is find a short poem, or one verse from a longer one to work on. You need 4–6 lines and the lines should end-rhyme – the rhyming words being the last word on each line.

✳ Copy out your chosen lines, with its title, leaving out all the vowels as you do so. And of course, write it as prose, with none of the poem's line-breaks. Include all the punctuation.

✳ Each pair should have a different poem to copy and when you are all ready, swap papers to see who can correctly insert all the vowels and set the poem out in its proper lines.

The day is past, the sun is set,
And the white stars are in the sky;
While the long grass with dew is wet,
And through the air the bats now fly.

    Cracking English Grammar in KS2 by David Horner

The Ox and the Snaik

...To The Big Ox

All hale! thou mighty annimil – all hale!

I wonder if it hurts yu much to be so big,
And if yu grode it in a month or so.
I spose wen yu was young tha didn't gin
Yu skim milk but all the creme yu could stuff
Into yore little stummick, jest to see
How big yu'd grow.

Anonymous

...To Snaik

Stoopenjus inseck! marvellous annimile!
You are no doubt seven thousand yeres
Old, and have a considerable of a
Family sneekin' round thru the tall
Gras in Africa, a eetin up little greezy
Piggers, and wishin' they was biggir.

You are so mighty long, I shud think
If your tale was kold, yure hed
Woodent no it till the next day,
But it's hard to tell; snaix is snaix.

Anonymous

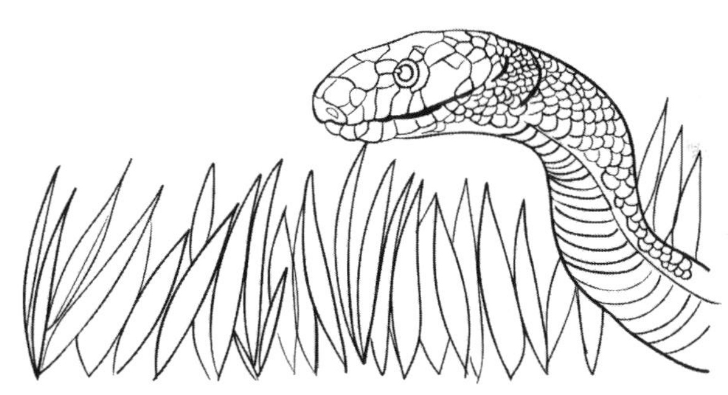

Spelling

The pieces you've just read come from two much longer poems. They were published in an American newspaper around 1850.

We don't actually know who wrote them. It is possible it was the same person each time, but whoever it was DID know how to spell correctly. They just chose to spell certain words wrongly – to get the readers' attention, and to make the writing sound like spoken English when read out loud. Try it for yourself – with an American accent if you can!

You probably read those two pieces quite easily and enjoyed teasing out the meanings from the misspellings. We all read better than we spell – but we also spell better than we think we do! You know about 10,000 words by the time you are eight – and just 26 letters make all their sounds!

Now it's your turn

Here is a part from a different poem. Once again, we don't know the author, but in it a sailor tells of his sad tale about being shipwrecked and swallowed by a crocodile:

> This crocodile being very old, one day, alas, he died;
> He was ten long years a-getting cold, he was so long and wide.
> His skin was eight miles thick, I'm sure, or very near about,
> For I was full ten years or more a-cutting my way out.

✳ Read the verse out loud to yourself and start looking for spellings to change.

✳ Remember, whoever wrote the poems to the ox and the snake didn't misspell every word. So, only change the words you think best create the sound of a word but still let your reader understand and enjoy your writing.

✳ Crocodile has to be your first word to play around with. So, Krokodial? Ckrockadiyl? English has lots of ways of making the same sounds, so experiment with different changes, then make your choice each time. Start copying the verse out, making your changes as you go.

✳ Now you've worked on someone else's writing, it's time to create your own! Choose any animal you like or admire – a pet, a wild creature or even one that is extinct! – and write a poem to it including some great – and different spellings.

        Cracking English Grammar in KS2 by David Horner

A Spell to Make a Rainbow

Using fronted adverbials

This is part of Charlie's rainbow-making spell, with his ingredients for blue, indigo and violet. His spell has seven lines all together – one for each of the rainbow's colours. He had seven different ways of starting each line.

Next	After that	Later	And now	Finally	Then	First

Each of them is an **adverb** or **adverbial phrase** and because each one comes at the start (or front) of the sentence, it is called a **fronted adverbial** and has a comma straight after it.

You can see in Charlie's spell that he never mentions the colour itself in each line. Instead, he chooses two different things that are that colour and leaves the rest to his reader's imagination.

Now it's your turn

✳   On the left side of your page, write down each of those seven adverbials, one under the other. Spread them out down the page, so the rest of your writing doesn't get squashed. There is not a correct right order, but obviously you don't want *Finally* first! Just choose an order that you think works well as a sequence.

✳   Think of two things, two ingredients, for every colour of the rainbow and begin to create your spell. Make your two things very different from one another if you can.

✳   Be sure to add details to your ingredients – quantities, measurements, descriptive adjectives, for example. These are called **expanded noun phrases** and your details will make each colour more vivid and create real interest for your reader.

Join your two ingredients together to make one sentence with the conjunction *and*. Remember, don't include the actual colour word in your lines!

Hint: You probably do know the colour sequence of the rainbow, but just in case, here's a well-known mnemonic so you never forget: *Richard Of York Gave Battle In Vain.*

   © Brilliant Publications Limited   Cracking English Grammar in KS2 by David Horner

Anagram-azing

An **anagram** is simply two different words or phrases made out of exactly the same letters. Examples: an anagram for 'listen' could be '<u>silent</u>' and an anagram for 'the eyes' is 'they see'. Some anagrams are really clever; for example, 'lost in space' also spells 'so let's panic' and the letters from the name 'William Shakespeare' can be arranged to make 'I am weakish speller'!

Anagrams

Every word in the dictionary is made from just 26 letters, so lots of our words make anagrams – though maybe not as clever as those above. Here now are four 2-line word puzzles for you. Line 1 is an anagram of a single word (one that can be tricky to spell) and line 2 is a clue to that word. Write Line 1 as a letter-patch, jumbling up the letters; see what you find and don't forget the clue:

Shy trio
>It's all in the past.

Rapid apes
>Can't be seen any more.

I shove music
>Because I'm rather naughty.

Brass mare
>Your face turns bright red.

How did you get on? The words are, history, disappear, mischievous, embarrass.

Now it's your turn

Have a dictionary ready and a list of tricky spellings if you have one.

To get you started, here are ten words with awkward spellings and before each one an anagram of their letters. To make the 2-line puzzle, first write down the anagram. Now, check the second word in your dictionary and use the definition to help you write the clue underneath.

Anagram	Spelling	Definition
lady cancel it	accidentally	
die, mince	medicine	
one quits	question	
not armpit	important	
buses sin	business	
a nice sun	nuisance	
your pint pot	opportunity	
pirate cape	appreciate	
have ice	achieve	
sure lie	leisure	

When you've tried some of these, see what anagrams you can make from words you struggle to spell correctly. Each clue is also a **mnemonic** to help you remember the spellings in the future.

   © Brilliant Publications Limited   Cracking English Grammar in KS2 by David Horner

Spelling

It is important that you can spell words, but it's even more important that you know what the words mean and how to use them properly.

For this activity you'll need a copy of the National Curriculum Spelling Word list for your school year (or any list of difficult words) and a thesaurus. You're going to choose words from the word list and create some neat, short poems around them.

The form chosen for this activity is the **kimo**. It comes from Israel and it is made of just three lines of 10, 7 and 6 syllables. So just 23 syllables altogether!

Now it's your turn

✳ Choose one word from your word list and make a kimo out of words that mean the same as your word. These words are called **synonyms**. Use a thesaurus to help you track them down – and don't forget the 10, 7, 6 syllables form!

Here are two examples:

<table>
<tr><td>

disappear

fade out, be quite out of sight, melt away,

be impossible to find,

do a vanishing trick.

</td><td>

mischievous

likes causing bother, naughty, unruly,

plays harmless tricks on people,

troublesome, rascally.

</td></tr>
</table>

Hint: Remember to put commas between each item in your kimo to separate them clearly.

Next, write a kimo using the word you are defining incorporated into the explanation sentence to show that you understand what it means. Again, here are two examples:

<table>
<tr><td>

experiment

To find out if something is right or wrong,

you just need to carry out

a good <u>experiment</u>.

</td><td>

recommend

If suddenly you get a bad toothache,

I <u>recommend</u> you visit

a dentist straight away.

</td></tr>
</table>

Hint: If this gets difficult, try writing your kimo in 3 lines of 10, 7, 6 words instead of syllables.

Did you ever hear a monkey count to eight,

    or arrive at school an hour late?

Did you ever eat a really sour sweet,

    or sit outside in a forty-degree heat?

Did you ever toast a really huge marshmallow,

    or scream when you stubbed your big right toe?

Yasmin

Spelling

Imagine a country where spelling doesn't exist, where you can't make spelling mistakes and therefore there's no need for spelling tests. Impossible? Well, it seems there are languages that don't have a word for 'spelling'. In Spain and Italy, for example, the idea barely exists! This is simply because in those countries a word's written letters almost always match the sound of the word – phonics.

The problem with English isn't that we are somehow short of letters. We make the same sound in lots of different ways. For example:

moo	**shoe**	**true**
two	**you**	**do**
stew	**through**	**flu**

Nine different ways of making the same sound! No wonder it takes you a bit longer to learn all the wonders of English spelling. Yet, somehow, we do learn it. Most of it. You read those nine words and probably thought little of your achievement.

Here's a writing game for you to celebrate the weird and wondrous ways of English spelling, and your growing understanding of it.

Look at the pairs of lines in the poem again. Each line is a clause linked by the word *or* to make one compound sentence. Little words like; *or, and, so,* and *but* that join clauses together are called **co-ordinating conjunctions**.

Have you spotted the other little trick in the writing? The rhyming words in each clause sound alike but aren't spelled alike. Look back and check.

Now it's your turn

* For each clause you'll need two rhyming words – with different spellings. So, *box* and *socks* is fine, but *box* and *fox* isn't as they have the same spelling.

* Each clause follows the same pattern, with line one starting *Did you ever ...* and line two beginning *or*. Now you're ready to write your couplet. Use with *box* and *socks* if you like.

* Write as many as you like. Perhaps build up a collection over time as you spot new unalike rhyming words. Aim for an interesting mix of lines – some serious, some sad and some silly!

Hint: Don't forget the question mark to finish each couplet.

Two into One

Homonyms

Work with a partner on this activity, if you can. Take a look at the words below, one at a time. Think of what the word means to you and write a sentence using the word and then tell each other your ideas and sentences:

bat	letter	sink	second	right	spring	jam	wave	watch

How did that go? Did you always have similar ideas? Did you find you agreed on the words' meanings? Or sometimes did you disagree? So, for *bat*, did you think it was a small creature living in a cave, or was it a bit of cricket equipment?

Well if you agreed, you'd be right – and if you disagreed, you'd be doubly right! That is because those words are **homonyms** – they are words that look the same when written and sound the same when spoken, but which have two completely different meanings.

Now here are two riddles – and the answers are homonyms from the examples above:

I am very, very short;

I am valuable;

I pass in the blink of an eye;

I never lose and I never win;

count ten of me to launch a rocket;

I am an Olympic Silver Medal.

I am completely wet;

I am a hand in the air;

You can jump over me or dive into me;

I say hello to you;

when I reach land, I die

and I say goodbye.

          Cracking English Grammar in KS2 by David Horner

Now it's your turn

✳   Choose a homonym to work on – either from the table or one you have thought of.

✳   Research and write down the two meanings of your chosen word. If you have a partner, take one meaning each. Use your dictionary and thesaurus to help you research your meanings and synonyms.

✳   Now write down what your word does, where you find it, what it looks like. Then choose your best three or four ideas to keep and make into the lines of your riddle.

✳   You can see that in the two riddles above, the words speak for themselves, in what is called the first person: I am short, I am wet and so on. You can now do the same. Write down your ideas for each meaning of your word on alternate lines of your page, so the two meanings are nicely mixed up. This makes your word sound intriguing and the riddle trickier to solve.

Have you worked out which bits of the weather Anna is describing? Here they are – but not necessarily in the right order!

fog	cloud	frost	wind	rain	thunder	hail	sunshine

Kennings

Each of those lines is a **kenning**: a short phrase usually made up of two words, meant to bring everyday things to life. They've been used in writing since Anglo Saxon times – more than 1000 years ago. They would call a ship 'wave's-horse', the sea 'seal's field' and the sun became 'sky-candle'! Each kenning is therefore a metaphor – and also a short riddle.

The kenning is still used today. We wear 'body warmers'; we build things with 'earth movers'; we go on holiday in 'people carriers'.

In each of Anna's lines, she takes two words (both nouns) and puts them together to make one noun – or rather a noun phrase. She then joins the two nouns together with one tiny bit of punctuation, called a **hyphen**.

Cracking English Grammar in KS2 by David Horner

Now it's your turn

Read the details before you begin.

Anna's subject was the weather. Here are eight more subjects:

animals	parts of the head	electrical items	round things
clothing	transport	plants and trees	outer space

✳ Choose one of them – or one you've thought of yourself – and make a list of 6 to 8 items that belong to your subject. For instance, if you choose animals, you might begin with cat, whale, hedgehog. Now you need to make a kenning for each of them.

✳ To do this, think of one thing each of them does, a verb. So… a cat *laps* milk, a whale *blows* water out of its spout, a hedgehog can *turn* into a ball.

✳ Turn each of your verbs into a noun – usually by just adding *r* or *er* to the verb. Your cat becomes a *milk-lapper*, the whale's a *water-blower*, the hedgehog is a *ball-turner*.

✳ Repeat this process for each item in your list and your kennings collection is complete. Decide on the best order for your kennings. Make a final draft with your subject at the top as your title.

A Day in the Life of... a Cloud

Thursday

Before 6.00 am, I descended from the sky and blocked the vision of people in Finland. By 8.30, I was creeping across the border into Sweden until, in my gloomy blanket, I glided out over the Norwegian Sea. During the morning, the wild wind took me to Iceland. At lunchtime I stopped to watch a football match there. In the afternoon I glided on to snowy Canada. After that, I rested in Alaska, ready to watch my good friend the Sun go down.

Morgan

Prepositions of time

A lot of people keep a diary, but what if the weather kept one? That's the idea Morgan has played with in his *A Day in the Life of a Cloud* text.

Look back to Morgan's diary entry and draw a ring around all of the **prepositions of times** he uses. Here they are again:

after	in	during	by	until	at	before

Getting the right preposition is very important. It helps make our writing clear and understandable to the reader. For example, imagine the confusion if a friend sends you some messages saying when to meet up. One message says *before* five o'clock; one says, *at* five o'clock and one says *after* five o'clock.

     Cracking English Grammar in KS2 by David Horner

Now it's your turn

Before you begin, make sure you have access to an atlas or online map of the World.

You are going to write a one-day diary entry for your chosen weather. The challenge is to see how many prepositions of time you can include in your writing.

✳ Choose one weather type for your own imaginary diary entry:

rainbow	snow	thunder	north wind	fog	sun	lightning	rain

✳ Open your atlas or look at your online map.

✳ Decide on a route your weather will take across the world.

✳ Write the diary entry, describing your one-day journey in the first person. As well as all the times, include the names of countries, oceans, rivers you cross and the sights you see below you.

Hint: You have been able to use prepositions correctly for a long time. Just try saying, *at Sunday* or *in three o'clock* or *on teatime*. They will seem very strange – and wrong – to you. So, read your writing out loud to yourself, to make sure each preposition feels correct.

A Gem of a Piece

foot,
flat, bony,
standing, running, dancing,
neatly, sweatily, colourfully, wildly,
rolling, bouncing, scoring,
hard, round,
ball.

Diamantes

The shape of this writing is clearly a diamond. And that's its name – or rather, because it is believed to be from Italy – a **diamante**.

Now it's your turn

There are different ways of writing diamantes, but we have chosen this way, to get the most out of the form:

If you look at the first and last lines of that diamante, you'll see the two words put together make one word – football – **a compound noun**.

✳ Choose your own compound noun. You can use one of the examples below, or one you have thought of yourself:

butterfly	skyscraper	earthworm	weekend	eardrum	teacup

✳ Write the two halves of your compound down as Lines 1 and 7, one at the top and one at the bottom, leaving space in between for Lines 2 – 6.

✳ Now write the remaining lines, following the instructions below:
   * Line 2: write two adjectives to describe the noun in line 1.
   * Line 3: write three verbs saying what your noun can do. These must be in the progressive, the *-ing* form.
   * Line 4: write two adverbs to go with those three verbs.
   * Line 5: write three verbs saying what the noun at the end of the diamante can do – again in the progressive form.

Now go back to Line 4 and add two more adverbs, this time to go with your verbs in Line 5.

   * Line 6: write two adjectives to describe the noun you are using in Line 7.

Hint: Don't worry about making the diamond shape straight away. Concentrate on choosing and forming the words you need. Save the shaping of the piece for your final draft.

                    Cracking English Grammar in KS2 by David Horner

Badger's Hexastich

Now that is a good title! It's also the name of a short form of poem. It was invented in the United States of America, but nobody is quite sure by whom. *Hexa* is a classical Greek word for six; it is used in our English word *hexagon* (a six-sided geometric shape) and the **hexastich** has six lines, with 2, 4, 6, 6, 4, 2, syllables in the sequence of lines.

Now it's your turn

You are going to write a *Badger's Hexastich* to explain something.

* You've spent a lot of time in school learning about punctuation and grammar, and you know lots of technical terms in these topics. So now, try explaining any bit of punctuation or grammar in the six lines and the 24 syllables allowed in a *Badger's Hexastich*.

* You could use your title to introduce your explanation, followed by a colon, for example:

> **Bullet Points Are:**
> big, fat
> dots, one before
> each item in a list
> or by key points. Useful
> instead of the
> numbers.

Or, you could use your title to lead straight into the poem. The title doesn't use up any of your syllable count, by the way.

> **A Passive Verb**
> is when
> you are doing
> nothing, but something is
> being done to you by
> someone or some-
> thing else.

Hint: Try saying the bits of your explanation to yourself in different ways. This will really help you get the syllable count right.

Do You Give In?

Everyone likes a good riddle, so here's one for you:

> What do you call a teddy with no clothes on?

Well? The answer is two words; two words that sound exactly the same:

> A bare bear.

What about these two?

> If your uncle is an ant, what is his wife called?
> Aunt Ant

> What do you call two pears?
> A pair of pears

Homophones

Each of these pairs of words is called a **homophone**. The two words sound the same when you say them, but when you write them down, each word is spelled differently and has its own meaning.

Now it's your turn

✳   First, read these pairs of homophones:

knight / night	horse / hoarse	male / mail
mist / missed	cheep / cheap	wail / whale

✳   Choose one pair you want to use for your first riddle. Think about each word on its own and note down a short description and any synonyms for your words. For example, in the very first riddle, a teddy is another word for a *bear*, and *bare* means wearing no clothes. Once you have done this, experiment with putting your ideas together into a question and your first riddle is done.

There are lots and lots of homophones, so keep looking for more to make into riddles to add to your homophone collection.

Here are two more (just for fun!). The answers are at the bottom of the page.

> What do you shout to a cat that's running away?

> How do you start a letter to Rudolph?

Pause paws   Dear Deer

   © Brilliant Publications Limited   Cracking English Grammar in KS2 by David Horner

Fifteen of the Best

I'm whispering to my book,
"A happy ending?"
"Or a sad?"

I am yelling to the moon,
"Just how far are you?"
"Can I reach?"

I am asking of this tree,
"So how old are you?"
"May I climb?"

Quinzaines

Why do you think this page has this title? Just count the syllables in each of these short pieces, and you'll see!

That's right, 15. The French word for fifteen is *quinze* and that's why this little form is called a **quinzaine**. Look again at the examples above and you'll see that each one is made of three lines of 7, 5 and 3 syllables.

As well as the syllable count, a quinzaine must have an introduction in Line 1, and two questions for Lines 2 and 3. Look at the examples again to see this.

Now it's your turn

Imagine you can ask two questions to any living creature or object.

✳   To start, decide on which creature or object you are going talk to.

✳   Now you're ready to write Line 1. You need a verb to show how you are talking – a thesaurus can help you here. Your verb must be in the progressive (the *-ing*) form. Finish the line by saying what you are talking to.

✳   Next, think about your two questions. Remember the syllable count, and when you have your ideas for each line, try saying them in different ways to get the 7, 5, 3 syllable count correct.

✳   Now punctuate your quinzaine:
Line 1: put a comma at the end of the line to show the sentence isn't finished and some direct speech is coming.

Lines 2 and 3: open your speech marks and start the talk with a capital letter. At the end of each line put in the question mark and close the speech marks.

Let's Make Lists

Not all of us can remember everything! That's why we make lists. And a list is where a **colon** comes in very handy. Lists and colons go together.

Colons

A **colon** is essentially two full stops – one on top of the other – and its main use is to introduce a list. Like these:

> You'll need these items: butter, sugar and flour.

> These are the pool rules: don't run, don't dive, enjoy yourself.

Making a list is easy – so long as you don't forget anything!

Shadorma

The **shadorma** is a Spanish six-line syllable poem. The syllable sequence is 3, 5, 3, 3, 7, 5. Here's an example of a shadorma poem written as a list by Abdul:

> **What to do at the seaside:**
> have a swim,
> build a sandcastle,
> eat ice-cream,
> find some shells,
> have a sunbathe in the heat,
> have a barbecue.

Now it's your turn

✳ Think of a subject for a list. For example:

my bedroom	a season	vegetables	makes of car	sports kit	my pencil case

✳ Choose one of these or one you've thought of yourself. Start by quickly noting down all the things you might include in a list about your subject. You will only need six for the poem, but a few more will give you choices.

✳ Write your subject as a title – with the colon after it to show it is introducing a list.

✳ Now write your six-line shadorma with one list-item on each line.

Hint: Try saying your ideas for lines in different ways to find the right syllable count.

      Cracking English Grammar in KS2 by David Horner

Mountains to Molehills

Now, a mountain is higher than a moor. And a moor is higher than a hill. And a hill is higher than a hillock. And a hillock is higher than a molehill. And a molehill is a lot higher than that wet ticket I slipped on. However, that ticket was going to take me off to somewhere I'd never been before.

That paragraph is built around those five words – *mountain, moor, hill, hillock, molehill* – words meaning things of different heights. This makes them synonyms – words with related, similar meanings.

No two words mean exactly the same – *big* isn't *massive* and *tiny* certainly isn't *infinitesimal*. Not the same then, just similar.

And it's because each synonym in that paragraph is only similar, and each new one is slightly less high than the one before, that the piece is able to create its effects.

Synonyms are usually adjectives. We've mentioned *big* and *tiny* and no doubt you can quickly think of some for *beautiful, strong, angry, bad*, and many more.

Synonyms for nouns are rarer but that's what those are in that first paragraph.

Now it's your turn

✳   Here are five more nouns. Choose one of them, or one you've thought of yourself.

a shout	a home	an animal	a river	a fear	an injury

✳   First, note down at least four synonyms for your chosen noun. This is the time to use your thesaurus. Next, put your synonyms into order: getting softer, smaller, less scary, less dangerous.

✳   Now you're ready to write your paragraph, using the sentence patterns in that opening paragraph as your model.

Do you remember that the final sentence in the model paragraph leaves us with just a hint of what happened next? To finish your own paragraph in the same way, write *However*, and add a last sentence detail to make your reader keen to know more.

You can leave your writing with that teasing ending, or maybe you now have the start to a full-length story you want to complete?

Simply ... Semicolons

A **haiku** is the most famous of the Japanese poetry forms, but there is a lesser-known form called **tanka**. This form of poetry has five lines with 5, 7, 5, 7, 7 syllables in the sequence.

You are going to try it out, but first a bit of punctuation to think about: the **semicolon**.

The semicolon is just a comma with a full stop on top. It has two main uses:
Firstly, in a list. If a list has short items, commas will do to divide things up. So:

> It was cold so I put on my coat, scarf, hat.

But if the items are longer and more detailed, use semi-colons instead. So:

> It was cold so I put on my heavy winter coat; my thickest and longest scarf; a big woolly hat with ear flaps.

Now it's your turn

Now write a list-tanka on any topic with four semicolons and one full stop. Our example is all about rain:

> Short April showers;
> drizzle, downpours, indoor play;
> thunder and lightning;
> welly boots for the puddles;
> cold drops dribbling down my neck.

The second use of the semicolon is to separate two or more sentences – but only if the sentences continue an idea or are closely connected in what they are about. As in these sentences:

> Rui isn't here; she's gone on holiday; Rohan and the whole family have gone.
> I need some new trainers; oh, and I'll need socks to go in them.
> It was a great movie; my mum loves comedies; we all laughed a lot.

You see how you don't need a capital letter after a semicolon? So why is there one before Rohan? That's easy – because it's a name!

Now write a tanka, made of two or three connected sentences, which need a semicolon between them. Like this one about moons:

> We have just one moon;
> the red planet Mars has two;
> sixty-seven moons
> orbit around Jupiter;
> Mercury and Venus – none.

        Cracking English Grammar in KS2 by David Horner

Now You See It!

- a group of them is called a paddling;
- a baby is called a duckling;
- an adult male is a drake;
- they eat grass, insects, nuts;
- they can live ten years;
- their feet are webbed;
- they build nests;
- they quack:
- ducks.

Here you have a sequence of nine lines. The first line is nine syllables and each line after has one syllable less, down to the one-syllable line, which also reveals the subject of the list of details. Clever, right?

Nonets

A piece of writing made in this way is called a **nonet**.

We've added some fancy bits of punctuation to the text – to make it look even fancier! Look at the different types of punctuation throughout the text: They are:

- bullet points – these introduce items in a list, rather than numbers or letters;
- semicolons – these come after items in a list, when each item is more than a single word;
- colon – this bit of punctuation introduces a list or, as here, explains what's gone before.

Now it's your turn

✳ Choose a one-syllable subject for your nonet. Perhaps one of these, or one you have thought of yourself:

toast	socks	maths	Mars	rain	break	bikes

✳ Do some thinking, and a bit of research, then collect bits of information on your subject. Note these bits down.

✳ Write the numbers 1–9 down the left side of your page and write your one-syllable subject beside the number nine. Choose items from your bits of information and make each one into the eight remaining lines of your nonet. Each line must have its correct number of syllables, so try saying each item in different ways to get the syllable count right each time.

✳ When you are happy with your nine lines, make a final draft of your nonet, without any numbers, but with all the punctuation in place.

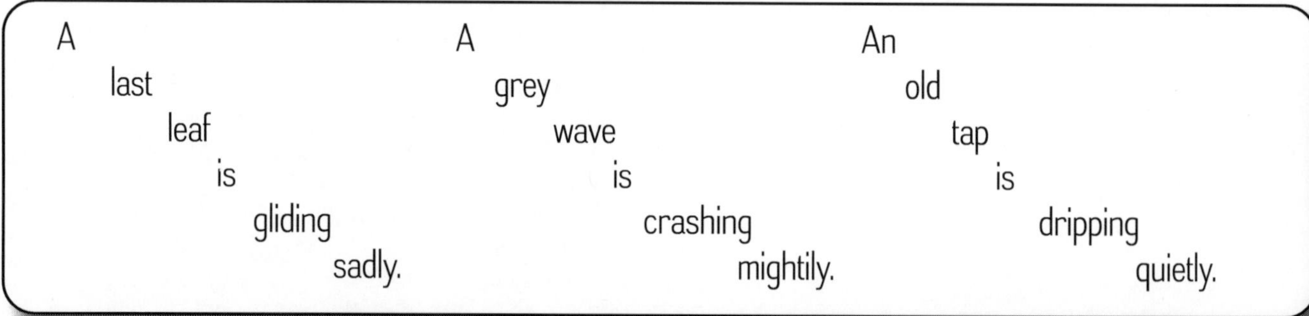

Shape poems

Poems like this are called **shape poems**. The shape of the lines coming down the page matches the three sentences which describe things also coming down. The setting out of the lines makes a picture of what the lines are saying. This kind of shape poem is therefore called a **pictorial**.

Now it's your turn

✳   First, choose three things that can come down. For example:

raindrop	helicopter	waterfall	window blind	bird	Santa Claus

'Things' in a sentence are called nouns. You can choose from these nouns/things or use ideas of your own. You can use a thesaurus to help you find just the words you want.

✳   Each of your three pictorial lines has the same six-word sentence pattern. Read these details carefully to create the right pattern:

Line 1: This is always *A* or *An*.

Line 2: This is always an adjective – one you think goes really well with the thing you are describing. Go back and check Line 1: *a* before an adjective starting with a consonant, but *an* if the adjective starts with a vowel.

Line 3: Now write your noun after your adjective.

Line 4: Easy – this is always *is*. The only word you can repeat!

Line 5: Time for the verb in the sentence – again one that you feel catches the movement of the thing. And because of that is, your verb has to be in the progressive – the *-ing* form.

Line 6: Finally, add an adverb – one to fix the mood of the line you've made. All you need to do to make your adverb is choose an adjective and add *ly*.

If you've like writing this pictorial, why not try another about things going up? Such as the sun, a flower or a rocket.

Here's a line to get you started:

Outside, Inside

Two large
slices
of buttered, brown
bread.
    Squidgy,
    warm egg,
    pale yellow
    and white.

        Thick, yellow
          skin
        that is peeled away.

          Soft, sweet
         flesh, curved
           like a boomerang.

               Jenny

Septolet

An egg sandwich and a banana – brought to life in just 14 words! A poem written like this is called a **septolet**. They have two halves, each half has just seven words, put together to make a complete picture. As you can see in these septolets, one half is about the outside of a food and one half is about its inside.

Now it's your turn

✳ Choose a food for your septolet – one with an interesting outside and an interesting inside! You can use one from this list, or one of your own:

a bowl of porridge	a hot dog	a boiled egg	a melon	a birthday cake	a fish-shop fish

✳ Write down your food and then add all the details you can to build a good picture for your readers – so they can almost taste it for themselves! You will also be making some really good expanded noun phrases.

✳ Now, get each half of your septolet into exactly seven words. Try saying your ideas in different ways to get this right.

✳ Finally, write your septolet out as a poem, so you like the look as well as the sound of it.

Hint: Remember to put a comma between your adjectives; start each half with a capital letter and put full stops at the ends.

Super-cinquains

A **cinquain** is a short non-rhyming poem in five lines of 2, 4, 6, 8, 2 syllables – just 22 syllables in all. It was invented by an American with a fun name – Adelaide Crapsey.

Here are two of her poems:

Hedgehog:
shy one;
small, secretive;
shuffling round our garden;
it's like a special guest has come;
timid.

The Old Railway Tunnel:
black hole;
grim, cold, empty;
water dripping gently;
it feels like a gigantic trap;
endless.

Now it's your turn

You're not going to write any old cinquain – yours will be a super-cinquain – packed full of grammar goodies in a single sophisticated sentence!

The subject of your super-cinquain is either an animal or a place.

Each line of your cinquain will be a detail of your chosen subject to build up an overall picture. For each of the cinquain's five lines, as well as the syllable count, you'll be given a grammar and punctuation task.

✱ First, write your title – the name of your chosen animal or place. Add a colon after it, so the title introduces the poem's list of details.

✱ Line 1: 2 syllables. One or two words only to introduce your subject. These words should be one or two nouns, or an adjective and a noun. If necessary, put a comma between them and definitely put a semicolon after them.

✱ Line 2: 4 syllables. One, two or maybe three adjectives to describe your subject. Again, put commas between adjectives and a semicolon at the end of the line.

   Cracking English Grammar in KS2 by David Horner

✳ Line 3: 6 syllables. Now you need a verb – in the progressive (*-ing*) form, saying something your animal is doing or something happening in your place. Use an adverb with the verb, plus another semicolon.

✳ Line 4: 8 syllables. Write a line to show how your subject makes you feel. Include a simile if you can. Add one last semicolon.

✳ Line 5: 2 syllables. A one- or two-word synonym for your opening line. Add a full stop to finish.

Once complete, your super-cinquain should be a rich treat to read! It should be made up of: adjectives, nouns, adverbs, a colon, semicolons, commas, a full stop, a verb in the progressive (*-ing*) form, a simile and synonyms.

The Same – But Different

Homonyms

Take a look at these words:

ring	duck	foot	left	bark	match	trunk	well

If we ask you what they mean, what would you say?

ring – an item of jewellery worn on your finger / the noise a bell makes / a round object?

left – the opposite of right / another word for gone / all that remains?

Well, of course, you'd be right, whichever you say. That's because these words are **homonyms**. Words with the same spelling and sound, but several different meanings. There are over 6,000 of them in the English language!

Now it's your turn

You're going to write a two-part definition of a homonym – using a couple of Japanese poetic forms. The first form is called the **katauta**. Two katautas make one **sedoka**. The idea is that the sedoka looks at the same subject from two different viewpoints – ideal for our double-meaning homonyms!

✳ First, choose a homonym to work on – one from the examples above or one of your own.

✳ Begin by writing as much as you can – quickly – about each meaning of your word. If it helps, look up the definitions in a dictionary.

✳ Start shaping your material into its poetic form. And you won't have much room – each katauta is just three lines of 5, 7 and 7 syllables. This means just 19 syllables in each piece. So get editing!

✳ Say your ideas in different ways to yourself to get the syllable counts right.
Here's an example of two katautas making a sedoka using the word *park*:

> It has lots of grass.
> There are roundabouts and swings.
> It's where you meet all your friends.
>
> You go in the car
> to the supermarket, and
> then stop inside the white lines.

Hint: If you don't give your sedoka a title, you can use it as a riddle to challenge your friends! If you find syllable counting tricky, then write your sedoka in lines of 5, 7, 5 words instead.

    Cracking English Grammar in KS2 by David Horner

Japanese Lanterns

However, this activity could be called,

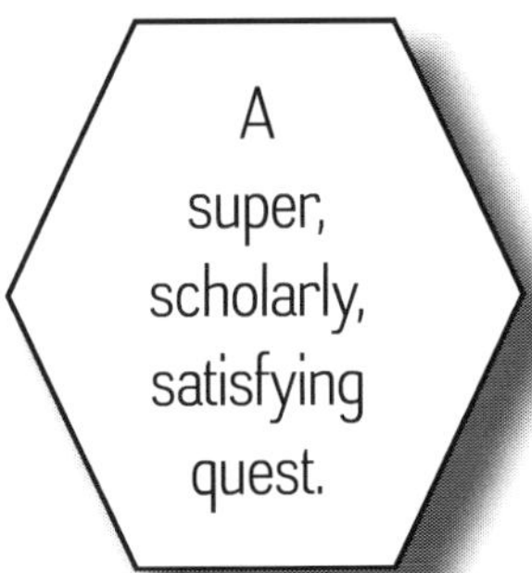

It makes a shape poem, written to look like a Japanese lantern. It's called a **lanturne**. Here's how it works:

If you count the syllables in each line, you'll find it goes 1 – 2 – 3 – 4 – 1. Count the beats in each one-word line and every beat is a syllable. So, lines 2, 3 and 4 go:

su – per (2 beats), schol – ar – ly (3 beats), sat – is – fy – ing (4 beats)

Now it's your turn

Have a dictionary handy, you'll need it a lot. You are going to write some lanturnes like this:

> Line 1 is always *A* or *An*
> Lines 2, 3 and 4 will always be adjectives
> Line 5 will be a noun to finish

You are going to write 2 lanturnes:
Lanturne 1 This must use 3 adjectives beginning with a vowel. So, *a, e, i, o* or *u.*

Because your adjectives start with vowels, your first one-syllable word will be *An.*
Your first adjective must have 2 syllables, your second 3 syllables and your fourth 4 syllables, each starting with your chosen vowel.

To end your lanturne, the last line must be an animal – a one-syllable animal, such as:
ape, bear, cat, snake, fox, pig or *owl.*

Lanturne 2

In this lanturne, the opening one-syllable word will be *A*, because now you will be choosing adjectives starting with a **consonant**. A consonant is simply any letter that isn't a vowel! Again, your adjectives need the right number of syllables – 2, 3, 4.

To complete your lanturne, again, choose a one-syllable animal.

Each lanturne is also an expanded noun phrase – here a noun with adjectives added.

Hint: Concentrate on finding the three adjectives in your dictionary. Don't worry about getting the lantern shape right until you set down your final draft.

Counting Creatures

Here's a tongue twister for you:

> **Three grey geese in a green field grazing.**

Say it slowly to yourself and then say it three times – quickly!

Expanded noun phrases

Now it's time to add some new, equally twisty lines to create a complete counting song – and each one a rather nifty **expanded noun phrase**.

Now it's your turn

✳ Down the left side of your page, write the numbers One to Ten. Write them all as words and don't forget to begin each one with a capital letter.

✳ After Three, write the rest of the twister given above. Spread the words across the page as you write them. This line now gives you the pattern for your nine new lines.

✳ For each new line, you'll need a different animal. Each animal has to start with a different letter. So, no gorillas or grasshoppers! Write your chosen creatures, two above and then the other seven below geese in the twister.

✳ The geese were in a field. Now think of nine different places for your creatures to be. Don't be afraid to use unlikely places – a bedroom, a library, a supermarket? Write your nine places above and below the word *field*.

✳ As an extra challenge, try to use nine different prepositions instead of repeating *in*. Such as *near*, *close to*. Write each preposition (plus *a*) above and below *in*.

There are four alliterating words in the twister: *grey*, *geese*, *green* and *grazing*. Therefore, to keep its pattern, for each new line you now need:

1. an adjective to describe the animal
2. an adjective to describe the place
3. finally, a verb saying what the creature is doing. The verb must have *-ing* added to it to make what's called its present participle. It also means that all the lines now rhyme!

Don't forget to use your dictionary for your alliterative word-hunting!

Hint 1: Be sure your first creature is a singular noun and the rest need to be made plural.

Hint 2: When writing each verb, remember that if the root verb ends in *e*, you take it off before making the present participle. So, for example, *freeze* becomes *freezing*.

  © Brilliant Publications Limited   Cracking English Grammar in KS2 by David Horner

How to be Rude – Like William Shakespeare!

We all know that being rude is wrong. However, William Shakespeare was rude all the time! In his plays, characters can often be heard saying very rude things to one another. Here are just five examples:

> Thou art a boil, a plague sore. (**King Lear**)
>
> You poor, base, rascally, cheating lack-linen mate! (**Henry IV Part 2**)
>
> Thou hast no more brain than I have in mine elbows. (**Troilus and Cressida**)
>
> ... a most notable coward, an infinite and endless liar, an hourly promise-breaker, the owner of no one good quality ... (**All's Well That Ends Well**)
>
> ... this leathern-jerkin, crystal-button, knot-pated, agatering, puke-stocking, caddis-garter, smooth-tongue, Spanish-pouch! (**Henry IV Part 1**)

They sound great even if we don't understand every word. Read them out loud and you'll see!

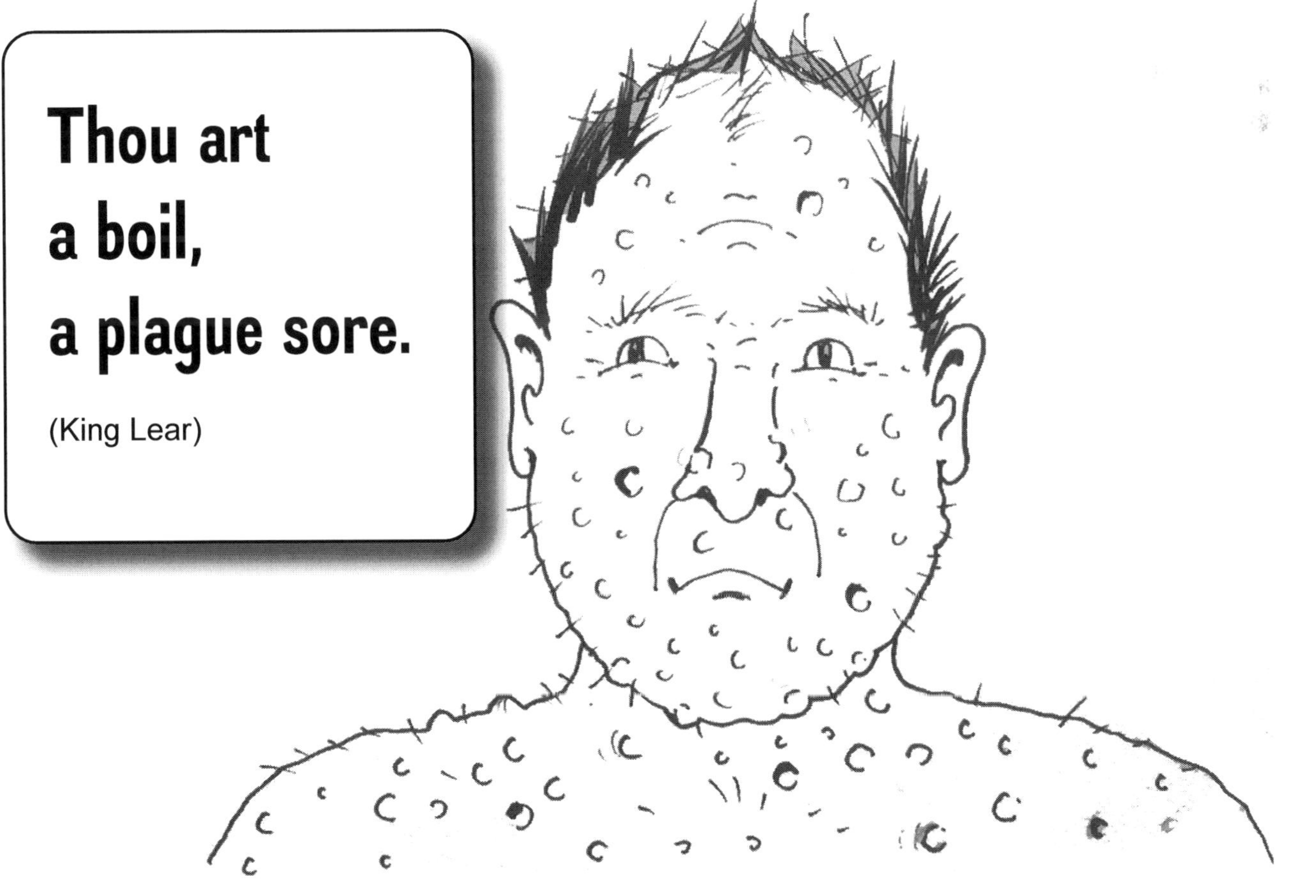

Now it's your turn

✳ To start your insult, write down *Thou art a…* – so you sound Shakespearean right away.

✳ Now, here are six word classes for you to find:

adjective	adjective	noun	verb	noun	noun

Look for each one in different parts of your dictionary. Leave some space between each word on the line as you write it down.

✳ Now add details to turn your six random words into a full-blown insult:

1. Add the suffix *-ly* to the first adjective to make it into an adverb.
2. Your second adjective needs a prefix and a suffix to make it sound unusual. Choose from these:

Prefixes:	anti-	dis-	non-	pre-	under-	mis-
Suffixes:	-able	-ful	-ic	-ious	-ised	-itive

3. Put a hyphen between the noun and verb and add the suffix *-ing* to the verb, so it is now in its progressive form. This makes an adjectival phrase.

4. Put a hyphen between the final two nouns to give you a simple noun phrase.

All of that gets you a very expanded noun phrase – and a splendid one-sentence insult, like these:

> Thou art an annoyingly mischeapful table-eating book-cloud.
>
> Thou art a rancidly antibottomless ear-sweeping basket-glass.

Make a number of insults and then perform them – mixing in some of those Shakespeare examples as well if you like!

    Cracking English Grammar in KS2 by David Horner

Lights, Camera, Action!

> It wobbles! It shines! It shakes!
> It sleeps in a cot!
> It tastes of sweet fruits!
> It wriggles and cries and drinks milk!
> It's great at parties!
> It has no hair and no teeth, and it wears a nappy!
> It's a Jelly Baby!

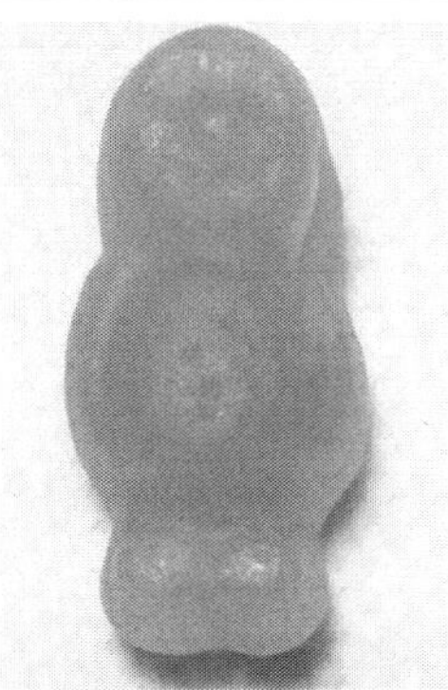

If a Jelly Baby was a real baby made from real jelly, and also an action-film character, maybe the above would be the poster for the film, or film advertisement! Those two words, jelly and baby, when put together become almost one word, and it's called a noun phrase.

Noun phrases

Here are some more two-word noun phrases:

hot dog	skeleton key	car boot	elbow room	clock face	water cycle	fish cake

Now it's your turn

Look at the noun phrases above. Choose one of these to be your film character.

* Write down your phrase as two very separate words. If you have a partner, work on one word each.

* The movie will be an action film and your character will star as an all-action figure. So now you need to concentrate on verbs: what does each of your words do? What does it look like? What exactly is it? Look in your dictionary and thesaurus for help here.

* Make your verbs into the lines for your movie poster or trailer.

* If you see your character as a made-up creature, like Jelly Baby, start your lines *It … ,* but if your character is a creature or person, start each line *She* or *He*. This is called writing in the third person.

* When you write your lines, mix them up to bring your character excitingly to life. Then, in your last line reveal the name of your character as in the example above.

Hint 1: Remember, this is meant to promote an action film, so feel free to use lots of exclamation marks!

When you have finished a rough draft of your writing, you could include your final draft in a poster for the film and include a film title and drawing of your character!

Making It Real

Fear is a trail-riding mountain bike dripping with fresh mud.
Excitement is a sudden clap of thunder in a clear blue sky.
Pain is a trumpet playing the same high note for ever.
Curiosity is a wizard's cloak covered in stars that twinkle.
Success is an oak tree, many centuries old and as wide as it is tall.

Nathan (extract)

Nouns are things that are real objects – things you touch, taste, hear, smell and see, but there are also things which are real that you experience inside you: moods and feelings. Just read the first words of Nathan's lines, and you'll see.

Concrete nouns and abstract nouns

Actual objects are called **concrete nouns**; those experiences are called **abstract nouns**.

In Nathan's writing, he took one abstract noun at a time and made it real by imagining it as a concrete noun – *fear* as a *bike*, *excitement* as a *clap of thunder*, etc. To make the abstract noun even more real, he added lots of vivid details to the concrete noun. Each line now becomes a rich metaphor.

Now it's your turn

There are lots and lots of abstract nouns. Here are just ten of them:

peace	pain	night-time	happiness	hope
sadness	laziness	amazement	fear	love

✳   Choose any of these nouns – including any of the ones Nathan used – for your own work. Now here are some kinds of concrete nouns:

a sea creature	a food	a building	a tool	a piece of furniture	an insect
a book	a piece of electrical equipment	a fairground ride	a soft toy	a flower	a vehicle

✳   Firstly, write down your chosen abstract noun and after it simply write *is*.

✳   Next, look at the examples of concrete nouns. Choose one – for example, a vehicle – and ask yourself exactly what vehicle the abstract noun would be? Nathan chose a *mountain bike*, didn't he? Now complete your line with your own concrete noun and those energising extra details. You can do as many lines as you have time for. If you think of different abstract nouns and concrete nouns to go with them, well go right ahead and make them all real!

          Cracking English Grammar in KS2 by David Horner

Small is Beautiful

List Haikus

One of the very smallest poetry forms is **haiku**. It's Japanese in origin and is made of three non-rhyming lines of 5, 7, 5 syllables. That might seem like hardly anything, but it's amazing how much you can squeeze into a small space!

For example:

> Mercury, Venus,
>
> Earth, Mars, Jupiter, Saturn,
>
> Uranus, Neptune.

You see? All eight planets – and in their correct order from The Sun! We can call this use of the form a **list haiku**.

Now it's your turn

∗   Now try a list haiku of your own. You can pick any topic – football teams, dinosaurs, weather, countries, foods – so long as you can fit them into the 5, 7, 5 syllable form.

∗   Finally, you are going to write two more haiku, this time featuring **synonyms** and **antonyms** – words that have the same or similar meanings, and words which have opposite or very different meanings.

Here's an example using synonyms for *big* and its antonym *little*:

You can make your haiku out of adjectives (like the pair above), verbs or nouns. Use a thesaurus to help your word collecting.

Hint 1: Don't forget to put commas to separate the words in your list haiku.

Totally Titles

The Freedom of the Relaxed Cucumber by Edith Spencer

The Eternity of the Hungry Sofa by Professor Dylan Robertson

The Sorrow of the Invisible Shopkeeper by Dame Alice Hitchens

The Naughtiness of the Rectangular Pig by Byron Munroe

Abstract, common and proper nouns

All of the above, completely made up, book titles begin with what's called an **abstract noun** – things our five senses can't experience, but things we feel inside us. Here are some more:

kindness	mercy	loneliness	guilt	dream
curiosity	anger	disappearance	bravery	love

Now it's your turn

Now you are going to create some excellent titles for books of your own. Here's how:

✳ First, choose an abstract noun from the list above. Begin your title with *The* and then add the noun. After the noun write the phrase *of the*.

✳ Next, you need a dictionary. Close your eyes and open it at any page. Write down the first adjective you find.

✳ Eyes closed again, open your dictionary at another page. Write down the first noun you find. This noun will probably be what is called a **concrete** or **common noun**. These are nouns for all the ordinary objects, animals and people in the world.

✳ Finally, you need an author for each title. Authors do change their names from time to time. These new names are called pen names. To make each of your pen names, look among the books in the room and for each of your titles, choose a first name from the author of one book and a surname from another book by a different author.

The wonderful Dr Seuss wasn't actually a doctor – his real name was Theodore Geisel. All names and terms like Dr are nouns too – **proper nouns**. You can add terms like Sir, General, Baroness or Professor to any of your authors if you like. These terms are also called titles.

    Cracking English Grammar in KS2 by David Horner

A Martian is Learning English

You come down from high in the sky.
Some humans wear you in their hair.
You are wet and cascade in droplets.
You're a scary ancient weapon.
Humans need an umbrella when you fall.
They make you with their shoelaces.
You cause floods if you're too hard.
An archer uses you every day.
What on earth are you?

Edith

Compound nouns

What is the English word that Edith's Martian is struggling to understand? Rainbow! The alien has never actually seen things here on Earth, so, sensibly it breaks that one long word into two short words to try to make sense of them. That word is a **compound noun**, a noun made by joining two words together to make one new word. Here are some more:

eardrum	rattlesnake	tablespoon	bookworm
watercolour	clockwise	butterfly	heartache

You won't have any difficulties with those words – you've been learning them since you were born. However, if you break each compound into its two parts, you can easily see the problems they could cause to a Martian.

Now it's your turn

✳   Choose a compound noun – from the ones above or one you've thought of.

✳   Write it down in its two separate parts. Write down what you know about each of the parts – what it does, what it looks like, where to find it and so on. The definitions in your dictionary might get you started.

✳   Imagine yourself as that Martian, looking hard at your compound noun. You are going to write directly to your noun, like Edith did, using you and you're. Include as many details in your poem as you like from your notes, mixing them all up as much as possible to make that ordinary compound noun appear wonderfully strange!

Hint: Writing like this, that speaks straight to someone or something, is called the **second person** form. It is also the form we are using to explain the activity on this page.

A Parcel of Punctuation

A bird.   A key.   A football fan.

What do these three have in common? When you write them down as words, they are all nouns.

Collective nouns

There is also a term for each group of those nouns:

a flock of birds,   a bunch of keys,   a crowd of football fans.

 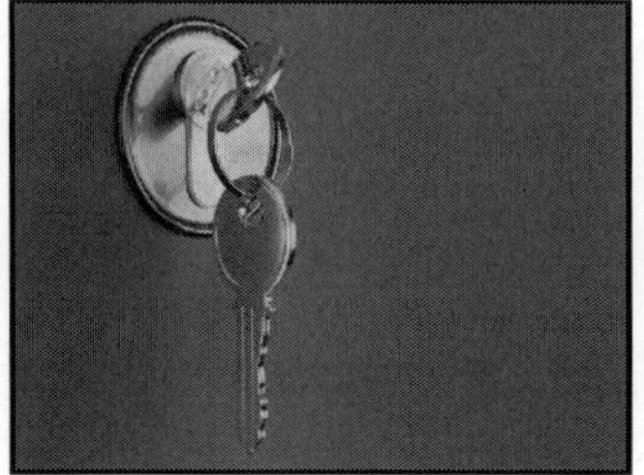 

These are called **collective nouns**.

There are lots of collective nouns for animals, objects and people. There are some unusual ones you may never have heard of like 'a bike of wasps', 'a stand of trees'. New collective nouns are made up all the time, like 'a network of computers', 'a click of photographers'.

Now it's your turn

However, there aren't any collective nouns for punctuation – until now! For example, what would you name a group of full stops?

You are going to invent as many brand-new collective nouns for items of punctuation as you can.

✳   Decide on one bit of punctuation and jot down several in a group. What do they look like all together? What do they remind you of? What else could they be?
For example:
- a swarm of speech marks
- a bundle of exclamation marks
- a boom of bullet points

✳   Do the same for other punctuation that you know. There are almost twenty different punctuation items you could use.

✳   Once you've finished with punctuation, you could go on to make a 'casket of grammar' – some collective nouns you've invented for grammatical terms like for sentences, adverbs or tenses.

Also Known As ...

> My name is Rhys. Also known as ...
> Forever-Asking-What's-For-Tea,
> Always-Has-To-Win-At-Monopoly,
> Philip-Pullman's-His-Dark-Materials-Superfan,
> Take-Your-Elbows-Off-The-Table.
>
> Rhys

> Meet Bundle the Cat. Also known as ...
> Won't-Stop-Climbing-The-Lounge-Curtains,
> Goes-Out-Every-Midnight,
> Grew-One-Eye-Blue-And-One-Eye-Green,
> Disappeared-Just-Over-A-Year-Ago.
>
> Rachael

Hyphens

That's an awful lot of hyphens! Here's why: we use a **hyphen** to join two or three usually separate words together to make one word, leaving no spaces between the words. For example, 'sugar-free' and 'ten-year-old'.

We are using hyphens less often these days and we prefer to make a simple compound, such as 'skateboard' and 'makeup' or we leave the two words separate as in 'post office' and 'high school'.

However, there are times when a hyphen can make a lot of difference to what a sentence means! Try these two (almost identical) sentences and you will see:

My dad's an old-car salesman. Or: My dad's an old car salesman.

Is your hotel dog friendly? Or: Is your hotel dog-friendly?

Some people have hyphenated names, such as 'John-Paul' and 'Lisa-Marie'. And Beyoncé was Beyoncé Knowles-Carter once upon a time.

Rhys and Rachael were playing with names. Rhys invented some hyphenated names for himself and Rachael did the same for her much missed cat.

Now it's your turn

✳ Begin by introducing yourself or pet with the real name and after it, Also known as ...

✳ Now you need new names – think of habits, likes, dislikes, funny ways, things you say a lot, things other people say. Then, as Rhys and Rachael did, turn each idea into a one-word name. Aim to make at least four new names, each with as many hyphens as you can cram in!

Pen Portraits

> Then, two pairs of speech marks curl into his mouth.
> Next, his beady eyes are made from two full stops.
> After that, his curly hair is created from thousands of apostrophes.
> Later, half a dozen exclamation marks make his jewelled crown.
>
> Elizabeth (extract)

Punctuation

Elizabeth called her completed piece 'Prince Punctuation' – and you can understand why! She started her pen portrait by drawing, and you are going to do the same.

This idea comes from the paintings by Giuseppe Arcimboldo. He lived and worked in Milan around 500 years ago. He created and painted imaginative portrait heads made entirely of objects such as fruits, vegetables, flowers, fish and books – but never, so far as we know, punctuation!

Now it's your turn

* At the top of a piece of plain paper, draw all the punctuation marks and symbols you know. Like Elizabeth, use these marks and symbols to create a portrait of a face – male or female, the choice is yours. Perhaps try a number of sketches to get one that pleases you most.

* Try to use every punctuation mark you know at least once, so you can include it in your written account.

* Now for the writing. Look back at Elizabeth's piece. You'll notice that she begins each one-line sentence with an **adverb** or **adverbial phrase**. Because each one comes at the start (or front) of a sentence, they are called **fronted adverbials**. These work really well to make the order in which she wants us to look at her drawing and understand what she's done. Here they are again, plus some more:

finally	next	afterwards	later	then	after that	first of all

Hint: Be sure to use them to create a correct sequence – you don't want *first of all* to start your last line!

* See if you can use them all to make a seven-line written pen portrait, with each line describing one part of the face and what punctuation you used to make it.

* Put your drawing and your writing together in the final draft of your punctuation-themed pen portrait.

      Cracking English Grammar in KS2 by David Horner

Punctuation

When you read a book, you can see the different bits of punctuation on the page, but what if, when the book is read aloud, you can hear the punctuation as well as the words.

There was once a comedian who came up with that very idea. He claimed on stage that if punctuation helps when we are reading silently, punctuation we can hear will help when we are being read to: a different sound for each different kind of punctuation. Of course, he didn't believe what he was saying for one moment; but he did know it would be very funny to listen to. He just made each sound with his mouth or his hand.

The comedian's name was Victor Borge; he called his idea 'Phonetic Pronunciation' and you can hear him performing it on YouTube.

Now it's your turn

You will need a partner for this task.

* Together, find some writing to work on. It could be a novel, a fairy tale, or a short story, but make sure it is a text with direct speech to give you a good variety of punctuation.

* Choose half a page of your chosen text to work on. You both need a copy of the same extract, so photocopy it if you can, or copy it out. No writing on the actual book!

* Go through your extract together and check the different kinds of punctuation. You need five or six different kinds: commas, speech marks, apostrophes, and so on.

* With crayons or highlighter pens, colour-code the punctuation on your copies with a different agreed colour for each different kind. For example, commas/green, speech marks/red , apostrophes/blue, and so on.

* Make a list of your different kinds of punctuation and now choose a different sound for each kind. You might have finger pops, lip smacks, hisses, tongue clicks – the choice is yours, but aim for a variety of sounds. See if you can make the sound fit the look of the item, and maybe use hand gestures to accompany certain sounds.

* Write your chosen sound on your list beside each kind of punctuation. Decide who will make each sound and start rehearsing!

If you have time, write a short, serious introduction to your performance, like Victor Borge did. This will make the comedy of your performance a real surprise – and get your audience laughing straight away!

The Punctuation Pals

Imagine a film company wants to make punctuation a bit more exciting by turning some bits into cartoon characters. They need your help, because you now know more about punctuation than most grown-ups do.

Punctuation round-up

You've learned 10–12 different bits of punctuation in school, but here you will focus on five in particular:

ellipsis	bullet points	hyphen	dash	brackets

Now it's your turn

✳ First, you have to design and draw each of those punctuation items as characters – facial features, body parts, first names too if you like.

✳ Second, the film company wants a cartoon-outline of the very first episode. In this episode these five characters introduce themselves. Also, and most importantly, each one will also explain what it does in a short sentence.

Here are the five types of punctuation to focus on, and their function:

- ellipsis: three dots to show words you might expect are missing: as in 'The Grand Old Duke of ...'. An ellipsis can also create suspense!

- bullet points: large dots ● (like this one or similar) put before items in a list – like the one you're reading now.

- hyphen: a small line put between two or more words to make one. A new-word-maker.

- dash: a small line to make you pause. Like this –

- brackets: two curved lines put round extra bits (usually small bits) in a sentence.

✳ You are going to make a six-box cartoon strip. Think of a title for this first episode and put it in the first box.

✳ You now have five boxes left, one for every punctuation-character.

✳ In each box draw your cartoon of the punctuation mark and give them a speech bubble. In the bubble the character says hello and describes what it does.

✳ In the caption to the box, write a short sentence showing the punctuation item in action.

      Cracking English Grammar in KS2 by David Horner

Greetings!

Speech bubbles

We have lots of ways of greeting people we meet. You might already have met a friend today and said *Hi*. You might have greeted a grown-up with *Good morning*.

In a comic or a picture book, if people meet each other, their greetings – and everything else they say – might appear on the page inside speech bubbles.

However, when you write a story, you don't want lots of large bubbles covering the page! So, instead, we add speech marks.

So, *Hi* becomes *"Hi."* and *Good morning* becomes *"Good morning."*

Now it's your turn

You are going to write a playscript – made up of lots of different greetings.

✻   Think of and collect all the greetings you can. To begin, just note all these greetings down.

Remember, people all around the world greet each other in their own languages. In France, they say *Bonjour*; in Spain it's *Hola*; in Greece, *Yassas*. Can you collect some foreign language greetings in your class and school?

✻   Illustrate your script. At the top of a page, draw two heads and beside each one a speech bubble with a greeting inside. Don't forget the punctuation – a capital letter to begin and a full stop to finish, ALL inside the speech bubble.

✻   Think of names for your two speakers. Start writing your script below your illustrations. Put the two names and their two greetings one under the other, with speech marks round them. Like this:

> Stefan: "Hello."
> Misha: "Hiya."

✻   Now add all the greetings you've collected, one under the other down the page – each fresh greeting with a new name and with its own speech marks round it.

We have lots of words and phrases for leaving someone. For example, *Cheerio* and *See you*. And don't forget other languages – *Farvel* in Danish, *Namaste* in Hindi, *Sayonara* in Japanese. Perhaps collect these and use them to make a second script with speech marks!

Grammatica Galaxy

Prefixes and direct speech

Here are six characters from a science-fiction text:

creature	robot	Martian	thing	alien	beast

Now, here are six almost-words, called prefixes, plus what each one means:

anti- against	**hyper-** extreme	**mega-** great
ultra- extraordinary	**macro-** massive	**micro-** very small

Now it's your turn

Make up six superwarriors for yourself by adding a different prefix to each of the characters, for example, *Ultrarobot*.

You are going to write a short story in which your six superwarriors meet in battle in the far away Grammatica Galaxy. As well as fighting, they are going to do some talking.
In a story this talking is called **direct speech**.

✳   On a fresh page, write each superwarrior down the left side on double spaced lines.

✳   Use a thesaurus and find two **synonyms** for each of the verbs: *shout, ask* and *say*. Write a different verb after each superwarrior. Put the suffix *ed* on the end of each verb to show your story is in the past tense, eg. *Ultrarobot bellow<u>ed</u>*.

The battle in Grammatica is so exhausting, the superwarriors only manage to say one word. They shout things like *Aargh* or *Eeek*. They ask things like *Uhg* or *What*. They say things like *Uh-oh* or *Ready* or *Phew*. Words like these are called **exclamations**. Exclamations are short utterances that you make when you are very surprised, upset or angry.

✳   After each of your six verbs put an exclamation from the ones above or ones you have thought of yourself, eg. Ultrarobot bellowed *What*

✳   Finally, punctuate your six lines. Like this:

1. Check each superwarrior name starts with a capital letter eg, *Ultrarobot*.
2. Put speech marks around each of the six exclamations, eg, *"What"*
3. Put a comma after each verb *shout, say, ask*, to show there's a small pause before the actual talking begins, eg, *Ultrarobot bellowed, "What"*
4. Check that each exclamation starts with a capital letter, eg, *"What"*. Direct speech always starts this way.
5. Finally, you have to put punctuation after each of the words spoken. This punctuation goes inside the closing speech marks. Remember, some superwarriors shout, some ask and some speak. So, now put two exclamation marks, two question marks or two full stops to end each sentence correctly, eg. *Ultrarobot yelled, "What??"*

✳   Remember, you are the storyteller. So, finally, use the lines between the direct speech to describe important moments in the great battle.

        Cracking English Grammar in KS2 by David Horner

Grow Your Own Word Garden

Syllables

A **syllable** is one sound or beat in a word. Count the beats in any word and you'll get the number of syllables. So, rose (1), pop-py (2), hy-a-cinth (3).

In this activity, you are only going to write words. However, each word you write has to have one syllable more than the word before it. Look again at the names of the three flowers above and you'll see the same pattern.

Now it's your turn

You are going to collect just four words at a time, growing from 1–4 syllables. Because the words grow bigger, a collection can be called a word-plant – and all your completed word-plants will make a word garden!

The words in your word-plants must be the same word classes – so four nouns, four adjectives and four verbs, but not a mixture.

✳   Choose a topic or subject for each word-plant to grow in your garden. Here are some suggestions:

Nouns	Verbs	Adjectives
vehicles	move	good
birds	make	hot
vegetables	see	strong

✳   Use your thesaurus if it helps you, and at first just jot down your words as you find them. When you have four you like, write them, in four, three, two and one syllable order, so it looks like a growing plant. For example, if your topic is wild animals, you might get *ant, giraffe, crocodile, rhinoceros*. As a word-plant, this becomes:

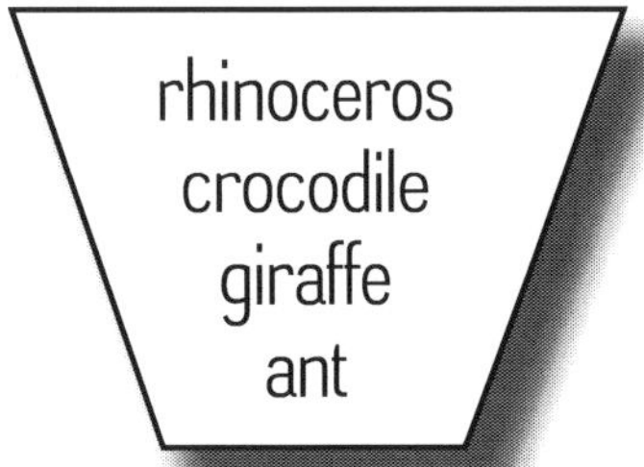

You can write any number of word-plants for each topic you choose and then set them all out in tidy rows in your very own word garden!

Making Nonsense Out of Sense

When people are asked to name their favourite poem, 'Daffodils' by William Wordsworth always makes it into the top ten. Quite an achievement for a poem written over 200 years ago!

Now it's your turn

You are going to turn that sensible, serious poem into a piece of pure nonsense! Here's how:

You need your copy of the poem's first two verses and a dictionary.

A nonsense poem needs nonsense words and you are going to make yours by using anagrams. An **anagram** is a word or phrase made out of the letters of another word or phrase. So for example, *schoolmaster* can become *the classroom*; *astronomer* makes *moon starer*, and *eleven plus two* also spells *twelve plus one*! Good, aren't they?

*   On your copy of the poem, underline all the nouns, verbs and adjectives. If you're not sure which word class a word belongs to, check in your dictionary.

*   Now, take those words you've underlined and, one at a time, jumble up their letters to make a new word – one definitely not in a dictionary. Start with the title. It can become *Foldalids* or *Didaloffs*, or any anagram you like the look and sound of.

*   For the underlined words, make a word-splat. Just write the word's letters in a jumbled-up patch. This at once helps you see different possibilities.

*   Write each new nonsense-anagram below the original word. Add, in between, the words you are keeping from Wordsworth's original text.

The poem has rhymes to end its lines. Lines 1 and 3 rhyme; Lines 2 and 4 rhyme; Lines 5 and 6 rhyme. When making your anagrams see how many rhymes you can make in your new words.

Hint: Don't try to make anagrams of all the words you've underlined. *Daffodils* can make lots of enjoyable anagrams; *high* won't make any.

Here is an example of what the opening two lines might become:

> I rawended yellon as a duloc
> that toalfs on high o'er laves and lilsh

Make a Soundscape

"Glug," gurgles the milk.
"Scratch," chatters the knife.
"Crunch," mutters the cereal.
"Scrape," squeals the spoon.
"Pop!" announces the toaster.
"Ssshhh," whispers the kettle.   Nathan

A landscape is a picture or a scene, full of things to look at. A **soundscape** is also a scene, but full of noises you hear and can listen to – like in Nathan's breakfast piece.

Now it's your turn

First, you need a subject or setting for your soundscape. For example:

on a bus	your bedroom	the weather	Christmas Day	the seaside	this classroom

* Choose one of these or one you've thought of yourself. Start by noting down all the different sounds and also what makes each sound in your chosen setting.

* Edit your collection of sounds down to the 6–8 you like most.

* Look back to Nathan's soundscape. He puts the sound itself first in every line to make each sound stand out. He also writes each 'saying' verb in the present tense. This makes the scene more dramatic, as if each sound is happening right now. The repeated pattern of the six sentences creates the overall rhythm.

Nathan uses a different 'saying' verb each time. Use your thesaurus if it helps, but think hard about which fresh verb you will choose to catch each sound.

Now you're ready to write out your soundscape, line by line. Here's how:
1. Write the sound-word – with a capital letter. It's the start of a sentence as well as the start of some direct speech. So, *Glug*
2. Put speech marks round that direct speech. So, *"Glug"*
3. Put a comma – or maybe an exclamation mark if it's a loud noise – inside the closing speech marks, to show there's a small pause before the sentence goes on. So, *"Glug,"*
4. Add the saying verb. Write it with a lower case first letter and be careful to give it its *s* at the end. So, *"Glug," gurgles.*
5. Complete your line with the thing making the noise. And of course, add a full stop to finish the sentence. So, *"Glug," gurgles the milk.*

Hint: Don't give your soundscape a title, so readers have to work out the scene for themselves.

Making Sense Out of Nonsense

Lewis Carroll's character Alice reads 'Jabberwocky' in the Looking-Glass House and says it's a strange poem, very pretty but… rather hard to understand, and that really, she couldn't make it out at all. The author himself said he didn't know the meaning of some of its words.

So it is those words, the ones that the author made up, that have made 'Jabberwocky' into probably the most famous nonsense poem in the world.

However, what if we've been getting the poem all wrong for 150 years? What if Lewis Carroll never meant to write those nonsense words in the first place? What if, instead, he meant to write everyday, sensible words, but he just wasn't very good at spelling? Or, when he checked his dictionary, he copied them down incorrectly?

Now it's your turn

You are going to look at all the nonsense words in the poem, one verse at a time.

Lewis Carroll's nonsense words are all either adjectives or nouns or verbs. Here are the ones in Verse 1:

Adjectives	Nouns	Verbs
brillig, slithy, mimsy, mome	toves, wabe, borogoves, raths	gyre, gimble, outgrabe

Look up these words, one at a time in your dictionary. You won't find them of course, so look around the page and choose a word that is there – one that is the same part of speech as the original. So, for *brillig* you'll need an adjective, for *toves* a noun (possibly plural) and so on.

Here is what Lines 1 and 2 of that first verse might become:

'Twas brillig, and the slithy toves
Did gyre and gimble in the wabe:

'Twas <u>breezy</u> and the <u>sleepy</u> <u>toes</u>
Did <u>jive</u> and <u>jiggle</u> in the <u>weed</u>.

There are lots of different possibilities, of course. Don't worry about making the lines rhyme. Just see how much new nonsense you can make by only using existing words. Enjoy your word-hunting!

Hint 1: If you're not sure if a word is nonsense, check to see if it is in your dictionary.

Hint 2: What if Lewis Carroll didn't even mean to call his poem, 'Jabberwocky'? He might have meant Jacket Wolf or Jammy Biscuit or …

  © Brilliant Publications Limited   Cracking English Grammar in KS2 by David Horner

London Bells

Oranges and lemons,
Say the bells of St. Clement's.

Maids in white aprons,
Say the bells of St. Cath'rine's.

Pancakes and fritters,
Say the bells of St. Peter's.

Two sticks and an apple,
Say the bells at Whitechapel.

Old Father Bald Pate
Say the slow bells at Aldgate.

Pokers and tongs,
Say the bells of St. John's.

Kettles and pans,
Say the bells of St Ann's.

You owe me five farthings,
Say the bells of St. Martin's.

Did you recognise that rhyme? You might have sung some of it when you were younger. The whole rhyme has fifteen of those small verses. It first appeared in a collection of children's rhymes called *Tommy Thumb's Pretty Song Book*, in 1744. The book itself is tiny – smaller than a smartphone! You can see it online in the British Library catalogue.

All fifteen verses, called **rhyming couplets**, feature churches in London. And not one of them uses speech marks! So, it's now time to bring that punctuation up to date.

Direct speech and speech marks

Let's start with speech marks. Look back at the first couplet: there should be speech marks around the spoken words. So: *Oranges and lemons* becomes *"Oranges and lemons"*

We also want a comma inside the closing speech marks. This gives a small pause and shows that the sentence isn't yet complete. So: *"Oranges and lemons,"*

And because the sentence isn't complete, *Say* should be written *say*. Finally, a full stop needs to be added at the end of the whole couplet.

Here now are more couplets, not from the original, and definitely not set in London!

"A sneeze and a sniff,"
croak the bells of Cardiff.

"Our tummies are full,"
groan the big bells at Hull.

"A bruise and a blister!"
shout the loud bells of Leicester.

These were written by Leon, after reading the original lines.

Now it's your turn

You are going to make up your own rhyme, like Leon's, using the correct punctuation.

✳ Choose three place-names to be included in your rhyme. You can use places where you live, or somewhere else in the country or in the whole world, or just select places from a road map.

✳ Start writing. Don't worry about getting perfect rhymes for your place-names. The original rhymes don't always rhyme exactly, do they? Have fun playing with different variations.

✳ See if you can use different 'saying' verbs to begin your second lines, as Leon did. For example, *cry*, *bellow* and *shriek*.

Aim to make your lines have the same rhythm as the ones you've read. Then your couplets too will imitate the tolling of church bells.

            Cracking English Grammar in KS2 by David Horner

A Song About Myself

A Song About Myself

There was a naughty boy,
A naughty boy was he,
He would not stop at home,
He could not quiet be –
He took
In his knapsack
A book
Full of vowels
And a shirt
With some towels –
A slight cap
For a night cap,
A hair brush,
Comb ditto,
New stockings,
For old ones
Would split O!
This knapsack
Tight at's back
He rivetted close
And followed his nose
To the North,
To the North,
And follow'd his nose
To the North.

John Keats

The third person

John Keats wrote that poem almost exactly 200 years ago. He was up in Scotland when he wrote it. He sent it – and three more in the same style – to his sister, in the same way we send postcards or text messages to friends and family today.

It's a very thin poem, isn't it? There's a term for poems with this shape; they are called **columns**. Today we mostly use the term to describe how newspaper articles are set out in columns.

One strange thing about this poem is the title; it includes the word *Myself*, so we expect the poem to be in the first person, using pronouns like *I*, *me*, *my*, but as soon as the poem starts, Keats goes to the third person, using *he* and *his*. He also uses the past tense – *was*, *could*, *took* and so on, as if imagining an adventure in the past.

Now it's your turn

You are going to write a column poem in the style of John Keats. Like Keats, you are going to write about yourself. However, you'll be imagining yourself as somebody else and therefore writing in the third person and in the past tense throughout.

✳ Write John Keats' title at the top of your page.

✳ Copy the poem's opening four lines – making some small but important changes as you go. First of all, change *Boy* to *Girl* if necessary.

✳ In Lines 2 and 4, Keats uses two adjectives, *naughty* and *quiet*. They work like opposites or **antonyms**. Choose your own adjectives for these lines, the first in Line 2 being one you think fits you exactly. For instance:

sporty	lively	bossy	chatty	busy	lazy	clever

or one you have thought of yourself.

✳ Begin Line 3, *She/He would not* – and end it with something you never do.

✳ Now add your second adjective to fit into Line 4, one that is definitely not you.

✳ In the long (and thinnest) part of his poem, Keats lists things he took with him in his knapsack (or rucksack). Start your own list to follow Lines 5 and 6 of what you took on your journey. Remember, only two or three words per line to make your column. Don't worry about including rhyme but if one comes to you – great!

✳ Use Keats' five-line ending for your poem. Where did you 'follow your nose' to? A place so good, you have to repeat it three times!

All Change!

> 'Twas in the month of Liverpool
> in the city of July,
> the snow was raining heavily,
> the streets were very dry.
> The flowers were sweetly singing,
> the birds were in full bloom,
> as I went down the cellar
> to sweep an upstairs room.

Re-writing poetry

Read the playground rhyme a few times to really enjoy its rhythms, rhymes and comedy.
You are now going to take over the rhyme and change it so much that you become the author of an (almost) brand new poem.

Now it's your turn

✳ The opening word *Twas* is short for *It was* but we don't use it today. So to bring things up to date and begin your re-write with the present tense abbreviation *It's* instead.

✳ Copy the rest of the first line, until you get to Liverpool. Change that to the city, town or village you are in. Unless you are in Liverpool, of course, then you can add any place you like!

✳ For Line 2, if you're not in a city, change it to the term that's correct for you. Then, change July to your current month.

✳ The next four lines feature comic contradictions – *raining snow*, *singing flowers*, etc. First of all, ignore the rhyme scheme. Instead, make up some brand-new lines, just as crazy and impossible, but using your own ideas. *Sunshine that rains*, *buses floating in the air*, *streetlamps creating darkness*, for example.

✳ Because your poem begins *It's,* that tells us that the time frame is in present tense, your new lines can be changed to the **present perfect tense**. To do this, you use *has/have*, plus what's called the **past participle** of each verb – it's usually (but not always) the root verb plus *ed*. So, for example:

> The sunshine has <u>rained</u>,
> The buses <u>have floated</u> past,
> The streetlamps <u>have made</u> everywhere dark.

Aim to write around five new lines – and keep going if you feel inspired!

✳ Finally, put your much-changed poem back into the present tense, starting *'As I go…'*.

Animal Antics

There's an old rhyme that begins 'Three little kittens have lost their mittens.' You're going to use that first line to make a quite different set of rhymes.

Now it's your turn

Down the left side of your page, write the numbers ten to one. Write the numbers as words and don't forget to start each number with a capital letter.

After *Three*, copy the opening line. This sentence now gives you the pattern for the nine new rhymes you are going to compose.

On a separate page, note down nine new animals to add to the kittens. When you have them, you now need to think of a noun that rhymes with your chosen animals. Just like the *kittens* and their *mittens*. So perhaps *snakes* and *cakes*. Don't worry if the rhymes aren't exact. Near-rhymes are fine. So maybe *snakes* and *bikes*.

In that original rhyme the main verb is written in the present perfect tense – *have lost*.
It has the auxiliary (or helping) verb – *have*
and then
the past participle of the main verb – *lose* changing to *lost*.

To go with your nine animals and nine rhyming nouns you need nine verbs, all in that present perfect tense. Usually to make a past participle, you just add *-d* or *-ed* to the end of the root verb. For example, 'gobble' changes to 'gobble<u>d</u>', 'jump' changes to 'jump<u>ed</u>'.

However, there are some verbs which change in other ways. They are called irregular verbs. Like *lose* to *lost*. Here's a few more:

catch/ caught	go/ gone	make/ made	ride/ ridden	freeze/ frozen	leave/ left

Don't worry about these oddballs. You've been learning them since you first heard English!

So, our snakes might make a line like:

> Ten hungry snakes <u>have gobbled</u> all the cakes.
> or
> Ten wicked snakes <u>have ridden</u> off on our bikes.

You have your animals and a rhyme for each, so now begin to create your nine lines – with nine animals, nine rhymes and nine verbs in the present perfect tense. Oh, and nine different adjectives to put before each of those animals.

Hint: Don't forget your last line is about just one animal. So, change the plural auxiliary verb *have* to the singular *has*.

Unfortunately/Fortunately

For this story-making game, you need a partner, one piece of paper, one pencil – and one dice.

Stories are made out of lots of things happening in sequence – some good, some bad. With your partner, you are going to make a story full of good and bad things happening – in just six sentences!

* First, write the title, *A Roller Coaster Day* at the top of your page.

* Below the title, down the left side of the page, now write the first words of your 6 sentences. At the start of Lines 1, 3 and 5 write *Unfortunately* and at the start of Lines 2, 4 and 6 write *Fortunately*.

* Next, be ready to write another word after all of those six openings.

* To find out what that word is, roll the dice. As soon as either 1, 2 or 3 show, stop and write the pronoun as shown below:

 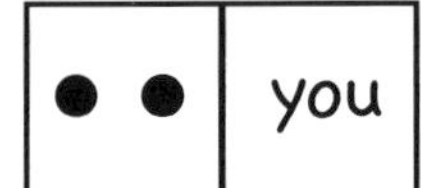 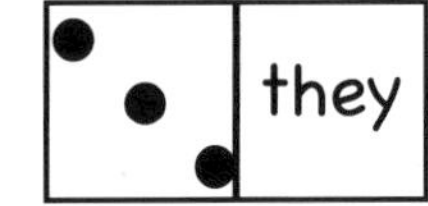

* Now you know you are going to tell your story in the first, second or third person.

* Roll the dice again, this time looking for 4, 5 or 6. When one of these numbers shows, write the appropriate verb after the pronoun:

 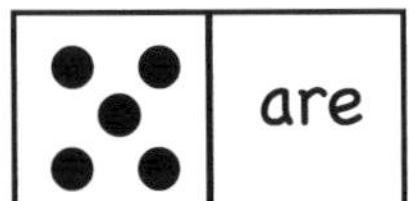 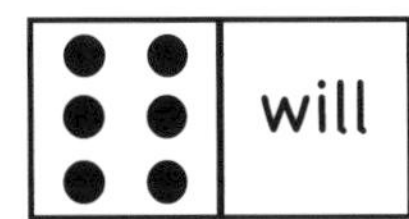

* Now you know you are going to tell your story in the past (yesterday) and in the past tense; in the present (today) and in the present tense; or in the future (tomorrow) and in the future tense.

* Talk together about what kind of story you want to make – a school story, science fiction, sport, adventure. But whatever you decide, get ready for it to turn comical! If you don't get the giggles, it's not working!

* Before you complete your six sentences, try saying lines out loud to each other. Do this a few times to practise and improve your six-sentence story-making skills. Write down the ones you think work best. Read these out loud to an audience if you can.

Hint: When you have got your six sentences as you want them, check you've finished each one with a full stop. And don't forget to pop a comma in after each *Unfortunately* and *Fortunately*, as in your sentences they are fronted adverbials.

A Dream Without a Joghopper

First of all, an awkward bathtub was cleaning a delumptious elbow.

Then, some favourite grobblesquirts hopped over iron kites.

Suddenly, lixivating magicians were nodding to outraged parachutes.

Later, quaggy rockets slept on tip-topple unicorns.

Finally, vermicious walking-sticks x-rayed yodelling zippfizzes.

(Class-made piece)

Fronted adverbials

Now, that is some dream! It is described in five very full sentences. Have you spotted a few Roald Dahl-invented words? There is also something else very different about these words. There's one for every letter of the alphabet – apart from j. That explains the title! The words are also in alphabetical order – check it and see!

First, see how each of the five sentences starts by setting a time. This is done with an adverb or, as in the first line, a three-word adverbial phrase. As these are put at the start of each sentence, they are called **fronted adverbials**. Five different ones are used to keep the writing fresh and always on the move.

Now it's your turn

Here are some more fronted adverbials:

At first	Soon	Next	At the end	After that	In the beginning	All at once

✳ Choose five for yourself from these – and those in the class-piece – and write each one to begin five new lines on your page. Take care with how you order them – you don't want to start with *At the end*!

All the five lines of the dream follow the same grammatical pattern, as here in line 1:

awkward	bathtub	was cleaning	delumptious	elbow
(adjective)	(noun)	(main verb)	(adjective)	(noun)

✳ Use a dictionary to find your 25 key words. Write them – the stranger the better, this is a dream after all – leaving space for the extra words you'll need to build your five found words into proper sentences.

✳ For a final draft, add a title, including its own word for the one letter your piece is without.

Hint: If possible, use the *Oxford Roald Dahl Dictionary* – and read all the details before you begin. Don't forget to put a comma after each of those fronted adverbials, too!

      Cracking English Grammar in KS2 by David Horner

This is How the Story Begins

> Under a blue, blue sky, there was a busy, busy city.
> In the busy, busy city, there was a high, high gate.
> Outside the high, high gate, there was a long, long road.
> Beyond the long, long road there was a hot, hot desert.
> In the hot, hot desert, there was a cool, cool oasis.
> And beside the cool, cool oasis ...

The beginning to each of those five (and a half) sentences is a phrase which is called a **fronted adverbial of place**. This is because it comes at the start (or front) of each sentence and it tells us the place where each sentence is happening.

Look again at just the first sentence above. It could have been written like this: *There was a busy, busy city under a blue, blue sky.* In fact, all the sentences could have been written that way round, all starting, *There was …*

However, by putting the **adverbial phrase** first, the reader is taken on an inviting journey from the vastness of the sky all the way to the cool oasis where the story proper will begin.

Now it's your turn

✳ You are going to write your own story-beginning in the same style. Here are six more story settings:

the top of a lighthouse	a tree-branch in a forest	the bottom of the ocean
a room in a castle	a garden shed	somewhere on a distant planet

✳ Choose one of these and imagine a number of stopping points before you reach it. In the opening above, the stopping points are the *sky*, a *city*, a *gate*, a *road*, the *desert* and finally the *oasis* where the story proper will start. Write your own four or five stopping points down, each one taking your reader nearer to where your actual story will begin.

✳ You will need a preposition to start each of your fronted adverbial phrases. The opening above had *Under, In, Outside* and *Beyond*, but there are lots more you can choose.

✳ That opening also had different adjectives to fit each stopping point – *blue, busy, high, long, hot* and *cool*. Each one gets written twice, so be sure you have a different one for each of your sentences.

Allan and Janet Ahlberg use this device in the opening to their picture book 'Funnybones', creating its mysterious setting before we meet those skeletons. See if you can find a copy and once you have your own opening, perhaps go on, like them, to tell a whole story.

Solo with Chorus

I am a book with a cover of blue,
We are the children that read it all through.

I am a ship with a wooden mast,
We are the waves that go rolling past.

I am a barn with a creaking door,
We are the mice that live under the floor.

I am a street in a great big town,
We are the people that walk up and down.

I am a wood, all green in the spring,
We are the birds that sing, that sing.

Rose Fyleman

  Cracking English Grammar in KS2 by David Horner

Solo with Chorus

Rose Fyleman was born in Nottingham. When she was young, she wanted to be a teacher or an opera singer. She didn't manage either of those ambitions, but she did become a popular children's writer in the first half of the last century.

'Solo with Chorus' a grand title for a short, simple poem, isn't it? However, the title does tell us how we might read the poem: one voice for all the first lines and more voices for all the second lines. Try reading the whole poem out loud with friends.

First person

The poem is written in what is called the **first person**. We use the first person when we write about ourselves. Like the poem, first person uses the pronouns *I* and *We*.

But the poet isn't writing about herself at all! She's writing as if she is all those things; she's imagining herself as each of them in turn.

To make the idea vivid she writes in the present tense – as if it is all happening right now.

Now it's your turn

✳   Like Rose Fyleman, you are going to write a poem made with pairs of lines. Line 1 always starts with the solo or singular *I am* … . Line 2 always starts with the chorus or plural *We are* … .

✳   Lines written as pairs are called **couplets**. Rose Fyleman uses rhyme to end all her couplets. Your challenge is to write couplets that don't rhyme. Concentrate instead on good ideas for your pairs of lines and good, sharp details to bring each to life.

✳   In her ten short lines, Rose imagines herself in an enjoyable range of disguises. For example, she's a singular *ship*, a *street* and a *wood*; she's plural *waves*, *mice* and *children*. Try to include an interesting variety yourself.

To get you started, here are some ideas for your solo/chorus lines:

piano/notes	pitch/white lines	car/wheels	cake/candles	field/sheep

✳   When you have finished your poem, rehearse and then perform your own Solo with Chorus.

Dinosaur Discovery!

The playfully perfect pyjamasaurus
The quietly quick queeniraptor
The really romantic raspberryonyx
The simply small-brained spoonatops
The terribly ticklish trumpetodon

(Extract from class-made collection)

Did you know, a new species of dinosaur is discovered almost every week of the year! Now you are about to find a lot more.

Now it's your turn

You are going to find a whole alphabet's worth of dinosaurs! Here's how:

✱ Look back at the extract at the top of the page. You will see that each line follows the pattern:

The + adverb + adjective + dinosaur

✱ Every time you reach a fresh letter of the alphabet, open your dictionary at that letter. Find two adjectives starting with that letter; put them together, making the first one an adverb by adding -ly to it.

✱ Look for a noun, also starting with the same letter. Find something a bit unusual – like the ones in the extract.

✱ To make your noun into your brand-new dinosaur, add a suffix (a bit added to the end of a word to change its meaning). There are five different suffixes in the extract and here are some more:

-dactylus	-ophysis	-osaura	-docus
-pondylus	-opteryx	-mimus	-nonychus

✱ Try reading the poem aloud, emphasising the alliteration.

Hint: When you get to X, don't worry, just look around *ex* to find your adjective, adverb and noun.

      Cracking English Grammar in KS2 by David Horner

Let's Go Gobblefunking!

Gobblefunking is what Roald Dahl's The BFG calls 'mucking about with words'. Roald Dahl himself was a great gobblefunker. He wrote words backwards as in Esio Trot; he smashed words into one another to make portmanteau words like churgle from chuckle and gurgle in Fantastic Mr Fox; he made up brand-new words such as gobblefunking itself.

Prefixes and suffixes

One of the things the BFG does a lot is change the beginnings and endings of words. So, we get mispise for 'despise' and disgustable for 'disgusting'. Those beginnings and endings are called **prefixes** and **suffixes**.

A **prefix** is any letter or letters stuck to the start of a word to make a new word. For example, un + kind = unkind; im + possible = impossible. A **suffix** is any letter or letters stuck on the end of a word to make a new word. So, use + ful = useful; king + dom = kingdom.

A **suffix** can also change a word from one part of speech to another. So, kind (adjective) can become kindly (adverb) or kindness (noun).

Now it's your turn

You are going to invent some brand-new verbs made out of nouns and adjectives.

✴   First, look at these four common prefixes:

de-	dis-	mis-	re-
delight, describe	disappear, disguise	mistake, mischief	recover, recognise

✴   Next, look at these four common verb-making suffixes:

-ate	-en	-ify	-ise
punctuate, hesitate	fasten, lengthen	terrify, purify	realise, surprise

✴   Now you're ready to invent your words! Open your dictionary at any page and pick a noun or an adjective you like the look of. Write it down and put one of those prefixes at the start and one of those suffixes at the end. So, for example, *mis + magical + ify* and *de + dollop + ise*. Try different arrangements until you find a favourite.

Aim to invent 8–10 new verbs. Decide what each one can mean. For example:

mismagicalify: perform tricks that never work properly.

dedollopise: take unwanted lumps out of food.

Write out your new verbs in alphabetical order, with a definition for each one and a sentence showing it being used. Who knows, perhaps one day one of your words will make it into the dictionary. That would be wondercrump!

Secret Languages

Children all over the world enjoy playing with their home languages – telling jokes, reciting rhymes, asking riddles – and even making up new secret languages. Here are two examples, from a book called *The Cat's Elbow: And Other Secret Languages* by Alvin Schwartz.

Syllables and prefixes

The first secret language comes from the city of Chernivtsi in Ukraine. It is called simply Ku and it's really all about syllables and prefixes.

Remember, a syllable is one sound in a word. So, judge (1), umpire (2), referee (3). Simply count the beats in a word and that's the number of syllables.

Now it's your turn

To speak and write in Ku, all you do is add the sound *ku* before each syllable. So, *ku* begins every word and forms a prefix and then gets added before all the remaining syllables in the word. For example:

> judge becomes <u>ku</u>judge
> umpire becomes <u>ku</u>um<u>ku</u>pire
> referee becomes <u>ku</u>ref<u>ku</u>er<u>ku</u>ee.

Practise using Ku by saying and writing your name. Next, see what your favourite sports teams or book titles become in Ku.

Hyphens and suffixes

The second secret language comes from the city of Albany in the USA. This one is called Iggity. This time you put the sound *iggity* after each syllable in a word, so that it also forms a suffix at the end of each word. If it helps you when you write, add a hyphen between each bit of the new word. For example:

Socks become socks-iggity
Trousers becomes trou-iggity-sers-iggity
Underpants becomes un-iggity-der-iggity-pants-iggity

Now it's your turn

Start to practise Iggity by saying and writing some of your family names. Then see what some of your favourite bands, TV shows and films become translated into Iggity.

Finally, to show off your new language skills, try one of these ideas using either Ku or Iggity – or both!

- ◆ Write and recite a nursery rhyme or short poem.
- ◆ With a partner, tell some Knock, Knock jokes.
- ◆ Write and perform a play scene for two characters struggling to understand each other.
- ◆ Explain to class members how Ku or Iggity works. Speak some of the language yourself and ask others to join in the fun!

  Cracking English Grammar in KS2 by David Horner

First Words

> **Slowly**
>
> Slowly the tide creeps up the sand,
> Slowly the shadows cross the land,
> Slowly the carthorse pulls his mile,
> Slowly the old man mounts the stile.
>
> Slowly the hands move round the clock,
> Slowly the dew dries on the dock,
> Slow is the snail – but slowest of all
> The green moss spreads on the old brick wall.
>
> **James Reeves**

By starting the poem with the same word on each line, the poet is almost telling us how to read the lines – slowly!

Fronted adverbials

The word *slowly* is an **adverb** and because it's placed first in the line, it is what's called a **fronted adverbial**.

However, in the last two lines there's a change: *Slowly* becomes *Slow*, changing the **adverb** to an **adjective**, and at the very end, *Slow* becomes *slowest* – the basic adjective becomes a **superlative adjective**, by adding the suffix *-est* to the adjective, it is used to describe an object which is at the upper or lower limit of a quality eg. *fin<u>est</u>, tall<u>est</u>, loud<u>est</u>*, etc.

Now it's your turn

You are going to write a two-verse poem, but instead of having just one adjective/adverb as James Reeves did, you will have two. A pair of adjectives with opposite meanings – **antonyms**.

✲   Choose one of these pairs of adjectives:

happy/sad	huge/tiny	soft/loud	light/heavy	wild/lazy	gentle/fierce

✲   Once you've chosen your pair of words, note each one down as adverb, basic adjective, and superlative adjective. So, for *slow* the antonyms are *quickly, quick, quickest*.

✲   All you need now are your four things that really suit your word. Think of four very different things if you can to make each line of your verse interesting.

✲   When you have your four things, look back at James Reeves' poem and write your own four-line verse in the same style as his.

Hint: Be careful when spelling adverbs. You don't always just add *ly* to the adjective. For example, happy becomes happily.

Five Super Senses!

> Thanks to my excellent ears, I can hear bees talking.
>
> As a result of my wonderful nose, I can smell the chocolate in Willy Wonka's factory.
>
> Due to my fantastic eyes, I can see right through castle walls.
>
> Because of my amazing tongue, I can taste ice cream even when I'm eating broccoli.
>
> On account of my mind-boggling hands, I can feel the red dust on Mars.
>
> Jamie

Most of us are fortunate to have five senses: *see*, *smell*, *taste*, *hear* and *touch*. But what if we had five Super Senses, able to sense anything and anywhere?

That's what Jamie imagined for his five-line poem. You've read all the things he would do with his super senses, but now look at how he begins each of his five lines.

Prepositional phrases

He starts each one with a different preposition or rather, because each is more than one word, they are called **prepositional phrases**. They make each line feel grand and important straight away. Here they are again, plus two more:

Because of	On account of	Through	Owing to	Due to	Thanks to	As a result of

Some prepositions say where something is happening (in, near, beside). Other prepositions say when something is happening (after, on, at). These prepositions say why something is happening.

Now it's your turn

* Choose any five of the prepositional phrases above and write them one under the other down your page.

* Add *my* and *eyes*, *nose*, *ears*, etc. to your lines. Put in a fresh adjectival synonym for *excellent* before each noun. As an extra challenge, can you use five different adjectives to the ones Jamie used? Use your thesaurus if it helps.

* Finally, complete the five lines with something each new super sensory power can do. Be as imaginative and extravagant as you can every time. Make each new super sense really exciting and enjoyable – for your readers as well as yourself.

Hint: Don't forget to put in a comma after each completed prepositional phrase.

 © Brilliant Publications Limited　　　　Cracking English Grammar in KS2 by David Horner

Happy Endings

This activity is linked to the one called Little Beginnings (page 84) which is all about prefixes – extra bits at the start of words; this one is about **suffixes** – extra bits at the end of words! Suffixes let us make new words very easily. Here are four words, each with a different suffix ending:

| wonderful | hopeless | embarrassment | dangerous |

These little bits really matter – if *hopeless* becomes *hopeful*, you have a totally different meaning.

You are going to create some suffix riddles, using the four suffixes above. First, here are more words using those suffixes:

grateful	restless	excitement	famous
beautiful	homeless	movement	mysterious
powerful	fearless	establishment	humorous
peaceful	endless	parliament	fabulous
wasteful	faultless	appointment	cautious

Now here are four suffix riddles for you to crack. The answer each time will be one of the words above.

What *-ful* is amazingly strong? _______________________

What *-less*, sadly, has nowhere to live? _______________________

What *-ment* is a visit to the doctor or the dentist? _______________________

What *-ous* is so good it may even be magical? _______________________

Now it's your turn

Write some suffix riddles! You can use just one of the suffixes above or write new riddles for all of them. If you think of fresh words using these suffixes, go ahead and use them. Use a dictionary to help you compose your clues.

Here are a few more suffixes for you to make even more riddles from:

| -al | -ish | -dom | -ian | -y |

Foxy Finishings

Suffixes

A suffix is a really useful way of making a new word. Usually a suffix is easy to spot with its distinctive spelling at the end of a word: eg. *-ive*, *-ly*, *-ed*, *-ing*, *-ish*. However, there are some suffixes which can be a bit tricky, simply because of how they are spelled. They come in pairs with only one letter different. Here are four pairs of the most common of these foxy finishings:

-able	-ible
likeable	horrible
unable	visible
believable	responsible
reliable	incredible
washable	illegible

-ance	-ence
nuisance	audience
ignorance	silence
importance	patience
balance	absence
distance	sentence

-tious	-cious
scrumptious	precious
cautious	delicious
superstitious	suspicious
infectious	spacious
ambitious	conscious

-tion	-sion
pollution	explosion
introduction	television
imagination	erosion
operation	division
nation	collision

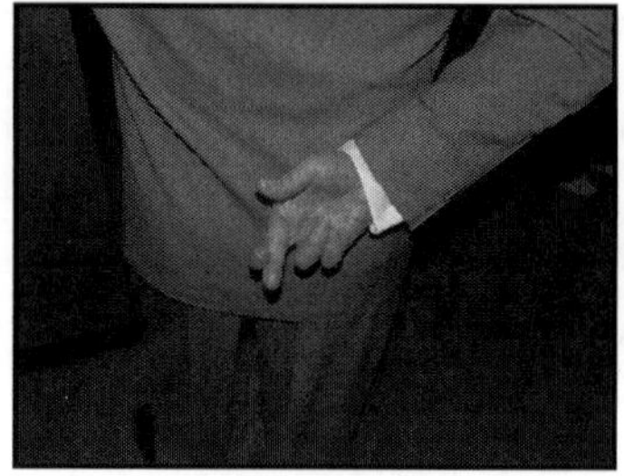

superstitious

suspicious

pollution

explosion

The suffixes in each pair even sound the same when you say them! Don't panic if you spell some of them wrong – lots of grown-ups still do!

          Cracking English Grammar in KS2 by David Horner

Here's a word game based on an old rhyming puzzle, the Riddle-Me-Ree. These are riddles in which every line gives a clue to the letters in a certain word.

These suffixes might be a problem to spell, but they sound so alike – they rhyme!
So, what four words has Dominic used from the examples above?

I fill the oceans with plastic when I finish with *-tion*.
I bang and send up sparks when I end with *-sion*.

I am easy to see when I end with *-ible*.
I can always be trusted when I finish with *-able*.

(The answers are at the bottom of the page.)

Now it's your turn

Make some Riddle-me-rees of your own!

✷   Choose two words at a time from any of the pairs in the tables and write a line for each, ending with the actual suffixes. Use a dictionary to check on the meanings of your words.

✷   Finally, here are three more pairs of suffixes for you to make more Riddle-me rees:

-er / -or	-ite / -ate	-ory / -ary

Pollution / explosion; visible / reliable

First and Last

I always hated warm milk
and held onto the glass for ages,
then kept its sickly taste in my mouth
as long as possible,
so I wouldn't have to feel it
sliding down my throat, making me shudder.

Looking through the windows
Into the four rooms
when the lights were switched on
and seeing all the tiny furniture,
especially the wooden piano,
that's why I really liked my dolls' house.

Isobel

There's a lot of detail packed into Isobel's two sentences! First, we learn about something she really loathed and then something she loved when she was younger.

There's another difference too, this time in the way each sentence is made. In the first sentence we learn straightaway what she is writing about – *the warm milk*. In the second sentence, we only know what she is describing – *the dolls' house* – right at the end.

There are names for these two types of sentence **Cumulative and periodic sentences**. The first sentence is a **cumulative sentence**. We get the subject in the opening main clause – *I always hated warm milk* – and all the details follow after.

The second is a **periodic sentence**. Here the subject and the main clause – *that's why I really liked my dolls' house* – comes last of all.

In a cumulative sentence we can build a growing picture with every detail we get. In a periodic sentence, we are kept waiting; the writer builds some suspense in us as the full meaning of the details won't be revealed until the very end.

Now it's your turn

✳   First, choose two subjects: one you like and one you dislike. They can be things you feel strongly about now, or as Isobel did, things remembered from earlier years. Here are some subjects to get you thinking:

clothes	tastes	places	weather	toys	journeys

Now write two sentences, one with the subject first followed by the details (cumulative) and one with the details first followed by the subject (periodic).

                                           Cracking English Grammar in KS2 by David Horner

It's Winter, It's Winter, It's Wonderful Winter

Poetry

That title is actually the first line of a poem by Kit Wright. You can find it in his book *Hot Dog and Other Poems*. You're going to use that line to go on and make a different poem of your own.

Your poem will celebrate all four seasons in four short verses.

Now it's your turn

✳	First, copy Kit Wright's line and then down your page write three more lines like it, one for spring, one for summer and one for autumn. Leave a few lines between each line you write. For each season, you'll need an adjective to match *wonderful winter*. Each adjective must start with the season's first letter and so it is alliterative.

✳	Next, you are going to add to each verse just two features that you feel fit that season. Each of the four verses will be just one sentence long.

This is because you'll be using a number of **conjunctions**. These are really useful words and phrases because they let us join short, simple sentences together to make interesting, good-looking longer ones. These are called **compound sentences**.

Here are your conjunctions:

when	and	because	since	now that	for	while	as

✳	Use each conjunction just once in your poem and then after each one, add your detail for the season. So, you might make a verse like this:

> It's winter, it's winter, it's wonderful winter,
> now that there are no leaves on the trees in the park,
> when there's frost on my bedroom window.

Hint: Add details to your lines to capture the feel of each season and make them enjoyable for your readers.

Joined-up Writing

Think back to two stories you knew when you were younger: *The Gingerbread Man* and *The Three Little Pigs.*

You'll remember that the Gingerbread Man runs away from his new parents, shouting:

And because the pigs won't let the wolf in, he shouts:

"Then I'll huff and I'll puff and I'll blow your house down!"

Commas and conjunctions

We have lots of ways of joining words and sentences together and in the examples above you see two of them. The Gingerbread Man's shout uses commas, while the wolf's threat uses the conjunction *and*. Read the two lines again and you'll see why.

By using commas, the sentence itself speeds up; we read it quickly to match the man's running. In contrast, the conjunctions make us read more slowly. The wolf's threat emphasises his power, the effort and strength he's going to put into his blowing.

 　　　　Cracking English Grammar in KS2 by David Horner

Now it's your turn

✷   Choose one pair of contrasts from the list below, or a pair you have thought of yourself:

thunder/lightning	gymnast/ weightlifter	iceberg/ snowflake	leaf/tree
roller coaster ups/ downs	elephant/small bird	butterfly/ windmill	giant/you

✷   Write a description for both words of your pair, using commas and conjunctions in alternate lines to create the lightness, speed and seeming effortlessness of one and the heaviness, slowness and strain of the other.

Here's an example contrasting a rocket launch and mission control:

> The rocket is still, silent, ready,
> > but in mission control the countdown goes slowly and steadily and endlessly.
>
> The rocket stands quietly, calmly, patiently.
> > In mission control they press buttons or look at screens or make notes.
>
> Zero and the rocket rises, climbs, disappears into the clear air.
> > In mission control they clap and cheer and hug each other.
>
> > > > > Matty

Here, Matty uses the three most common conjunctions – *and*, *but*, *or* – in his piece. You can use any or all of them. He also has adjectives, verbs and adverbs between his commas and conjunctions; if you can do the same, it will give your writing real variety.

Hint: Remember to use your thesaurus for your word-hunting.

Little Beginnings

In this game, you are going to create some riddles. But first, a quiz question: Look carefully at each of these words – can you spot what they have in common?

| dislike | incorrect | unwell | reappear |

They've all got different little bits at the beginning. Each of these little beginning bits is called a **prefix**. So, we can say that a prefix is a group of letters added to the start of a word to make a new word.

Prefixes

Here are some more words using the prefixes in the first list:

disgusting	infant	unimportant	remove
disaster	inland	uninteresting	repeat
disbelief	indoors	unhappy	return
disappear	incredible	untidy	recycle
dissatisfied	incomplete	unopened	recover

Look at the four riddles below. Each of the answers is one word – and the right word is among those above.

This *dis-* can vanish into thin air. ___________________

This *in-* describes a young child at school. ___________________

This *un-* is rather sad about something. ___________________

This *re-* takes things and makes them so you can use them again.

____

Now it's your turn

Now you're going to make your own riddles, like those in the examples.

✳   Write them using just one of the prefixes above or all of them.

✳   Here are some more prefixes that you can put before words to make more riddles:

| sub- | pre- | super- | under- | mid- |

Hint: Use your dictionary to find your words if it helps.

Growing, Growing, Grown!

Jack-
et pot-
a-to, fresh
from the oven,
with your thick, dark skin,
and your fluffy insides
stuffed full of sticky baked beans,
all topped with loads of grated cheese,
with golden, melted butter dribbling
down you, you are just perfect for my tea.

Syllables

Here the lines get a syllable longer each time, all the way to ten. Count them and see. This is called an **etheree**.

Now it's your turn

The etheree above begins, Jacket potato, which is a **noun phrase** – this is a noun made of more than one word, in this case just two words. Here are some more two-word noun phrases:

football match	apple crumble	musical chairs
rock pool	car park	disc jockey

✳   Choose one of the two-word noun phrases, or one you've thought of yourself, and write it to start your etheree. Make sure you count the syllables as you go!

Remember to put in a hyphen when you have to break a word in the middle, as in Jack- /et pot- /a-/to. This shows where the syllables are, and slows the reader down, making them curious about what is to come.

✳   Now you have your noun phrase opening, you're going to add all the details you can to bring your noun phrase subject to life. You can make notes of ideas on a separate piece of paper if it helps. Then experiment with different ways of saying these ideas to get them to fit into the syllabic form.

Have you noticed that our etheree is just one sentence long? Yours will be the same, making the original simple noun phrase into what's called an **expanded noun phrase**.

Good Day/Bad Day

Today will be a bad day for you. It will be windy and rainy all day. In school a friend will get you into trouble and for lunch it will be dry sausages with plastic skins. On TV you will only find programmes about improving homes. Before bed you will have to help put out the non-recycling bins.

Today will be a great day for you! After a frost, it will be chilly but then the sun will shine all day. School will let you wear PJs or football kit for the day and the only work will be PE and painting. A school friend will ask you to go on holiday with them. Tea will be only treat food and before bed you will watch the best ever episode of your favourite show.

Aarav and Joe

Lots of people like to look into the future. Some people visit fortune tellers, while others have their palms read and lots of us read our horoscopes in magazines and newspapers. Horoscopes claim to predict what lies in store for us, just like the ones written by Aarav and Joe.

Future tense

Because horoscopes are all about the future, they are always written with the verbs in the **future tense**. Each piece is written directly to the reader and it is done in the **second person** (you). Look back at the boys' writing and see how many examples you can find.

Now it's your turn

Like the boys' horoscopes, you are going to predict two very different days – a very bad one and a really good one!

* Begin each horoscope just like Aarav and Joe did and then go on to suggest what lies in store for each day. You can include the same subjects as theirs, plus any more you can think of.

* Aim to include at least five predictions for each day.

* Above all, whatever you predict for each day, don't forget it must all be done in the future tense and the second person.

      Cracking English Grammar in KS2 by David Horner

How to Start Your Novel

Lots of things go into the making of a good story. One of the most important things is an opening paragraph that grabs your reader straightaway. You can even play with words. Try this:

> She fell. In fact, she fell so far, she fellded. For a long, long time she falled and she felled. She thought she would never stop felling. It was more than a fallier fall, it had to be the falliest, felliest, fallingest fall ever. She might be about to become the greatest faller in the world.

Now, here's a fact about verbs: there are two kinds, regular and irregular. For example, *talk* is a **regular verb** – and here's why: if we meet right now, we *talk*; if we met yesterday, then we *talked*; and if you add have before it, you get we have *talked*. These changes make the verb's tenses. So, for all **regular verbs** – and almost all are regular – to change the tense, you just add *-ed*.

But **irregular verbs** are not so well behaved. If I swap *talk* for *speak*, the tenses become, we *speak*, we *spoke*, we have *spoken*. You don't find these things tricky, as you learned how to use them correctly when you first began talking.

That's exactly why that opening paragraph works – all that playing around with the simple verb *fall*. It appears ten times in different forms of made-up words across the paragraph. It starts just with *fell* but then the playing with the possible variations captures our interest and builds the drama.

Now it's your turn

Here are some more irregular verbs:

sing	break	grow	draw	take	sleep	write

✳ Choose one of them or one you've thought of yourself. Start by noting down all the ways you can think of to change the basic irregular verb. Go on to use the paragraph above as your model to begin your own opening.

✳ In the paragraph's last sentence, the verb becomes an adjective – *fallier, falliest, felliest, fallingest* and a noun too – *faller*. So now, do the same by making your own adjectives and nouns to complete your paragraph.

These groups of words are called **word families**.

✳ Try out a few opening paragraphs to get to one you really like – and maybe go on to develop the story. Who knows, you might get to complete a whole novel!

Little Things Mean a Lot!

Here's an old tongue twister:

> She sells seashells **on** the seashore.

How fast can you say it?

You'll have noticed that one word is highlighted: *on*. Words like these are called **prepositions**. They may be small, but they are really important in a sentence because they tell a reader where something is happening. So, choosing the right preposition matters: you do not want to write *up* when you mean *down*!

Prepositions

There are lots of prepositions – some are single words and some short phrases. Here are a few more:

above	to	far from	inside	under	behind
near	next to	by	close to	over	down

Now it's your turn

Game 1

✳ First, write that old tongue twister at the top of your page.

✳ Down the left side, below the word *She*, write the five pronouns *He, They, I, You, We* in any order.

✳ Below the preposition *on* write five different prepositions, each starting with a different letter.

✳ Each preposition now gives you the initial letter sound for your five new alliterating twisters. Your new twisters can be as silly as you like, but be sure you keep the sentence pattern of that first one:

pronoun + verb + noun + preposition + the + noun

For example, if you choose the preposition *into*, you might come up with

> They invite iguanas into the iceberg.

Cracking English Grammar in KS2 by David Horner

Game 2

Here's another tongue twister and this time the preposition comes first. That last twister needed four words to alliterate; this one has six:

> Round the rugged rocks the ragged rascals run.

Say it over and then copy it at the top of your page. Below Round, write another preposition, starting with a different letter. This gives you the letter sound for your first new twister. Again, use the pattern of the original line to make your new one:

preposition + the + adjective + noun + the + adjective + noun + verb

So, for example, if you chose beside, you might make *Beside the broken boulders the bouncy ball bobbles.*

See how many more you can make, beginning with those different prepositions. Remember to look in your dictionary for helpful words.

Finally, don't forget to see who's really good – and maybe not so good – at saying the new twisters.

> I went to the pictures tomorrow,
>   I took a front seat at the back.
> I fell from the pit to the gallery
>   and broke a front bone in my back.
> A lady she gave me chocolate,
>   I ate it and gave it her back.
> I phoned for a taxi and walked it
>   and that's why I never came back.

Past tense to future tense

That's an old playground rhyme, with a bit of nonsense in almost every line.

Look at the beginning of the rhyme: from the way the first line starts, we are all expecting it to end *last night* or *yesterday* or any time in the past. Instead, we get *tomorrow*. As grammar, the verb is in the past tense (*went*) but the noun is in the future (*tomorrow*).

And so the rhyme goes on, with the second part of most lines saying the opposite of the first part.

Now it's your turn

You are now going to play around with the rhyme by turning its timescale upside down, from the original into the opposite.

✳   Your first change will be to change the word *tomorrow* into a time in the past: *last Christmas* or *yesterday* or one you've thought of yourself.

✳   To keep the nonsense of the opening line, you now have to change that main verb from the past tense (*went*) into the future tense (*will go*). There are nine more main verbs, so don't miss any!

✳   Keep the rhyme scheme – it's just the same word *back* repeated four times.

✳   You can keep the same story too, if you wish. However, you can try changing some of the vocabulary of the original rhyme. So, you might begin your own version:

>   I will walk to the cinema yesterday

✳   You might also change details in the rhyme. So, rather than the *cinema*, it could a *bus* or a *funfair ride*. Include as many details of your own as you like, because each change you add makes the rhyme more your own.

        Cracking English Grammar in KS2 by David Horner

Sssssssshhhhhh – Silent Letters

Silent letters

Look at the words beside each letter below. Each word includes this letter, but it is silent.

A	head	**L**	talk
B	thumb	**N**	autumn
C	scissors	**O**	leopard
D	Wednesday	**P**	receipt
E	cake	**S**	island
G	sign	**T**	castle
H	hour	**U**	guess / autumn
I	suit	**W**	write / wrong
K	knight		

Amazing, eh? And these are just some examples – you can find lots more. We have 26 letters in our alphabet and three quarters of them appear in words where you can't even hear them!

Now here's one verse from a poem that gets these silent letters working:

As quiet as the k in knife,
as inaudible as the t in thistle,
as unheard as the b in crumb,
that's how silent it is on Mars.

Now it's your turn

✳ Note down some adjectives that are synonyms for *silent* – use a thesaurus to help you.

✳ Write three lines like the ones previously, using an *As … as …* **simile** in each one with your adjectival synonym in the middle; and to complete the line write your chosen silent letter and word.

✳ A verse like this, with four lines, is called a **quatrain**. For the fourth line begin, *that's how silent it is* and finish the line with someone, somewhere or something genuinely silent.

✳ Aim for three quatrains – using different adjectival synonyms, silent letters and endings in each one.

Sssssssshhhhhh – Letters Sleeping!

> What is quiet in listen,
> hushed in deliver,
> mum in business,
> soundless in muscle,
> completely silent in knowledge –
> and loves being played?

This kind of game is called an **enigma**. It is both a riddle and a short verse or poem. Enigmas were popular in the past, so let's hope you can have fun with them now.

Silent letters

Here's a list of silent letters – letters in words you can see but don't hear. This should be a big clue to solving that enigma!

A	beach	**L**	half
B	doubt	**N**	solemn
C	muscle	**O**	people
D	Wednesday	**P**	psychology
E	bruise	**R**	deliver
G	strength	**S**	debris
H	honest	**T**	listen
I	business	**U**	guitar
K	knowledge	**W**	answer

Now write the silent letter in the words ending lines 1–5 and they should spell
T-R-I-C-K. Line 6 gives you a final clue – this time to the meaning of the whole word.

    Cracking English Grammar in KS2 by David Horner

Now it's your turn

Begin by choosing a word of between four and six letters to be the subject of your enigma. Make sure you choose a word that only uses the letters in the list from the previous page.

✳ For your words with silent letters, use ones from the list, or ones you have thought of for yourself.

✳ Now note down some synonyms for *silent*. You need as many synonyms as the letters in your chosen word. Use a thesaurus to help you if needed.

✳ Write your enigma, with *What is* and then a letter-clue on each line. Start the final line *and* then add your clue to the whole word's meaning.

✳ Finally, write the solution to your enigma at the bottom of your page – upside down, so your readers can't cheat!

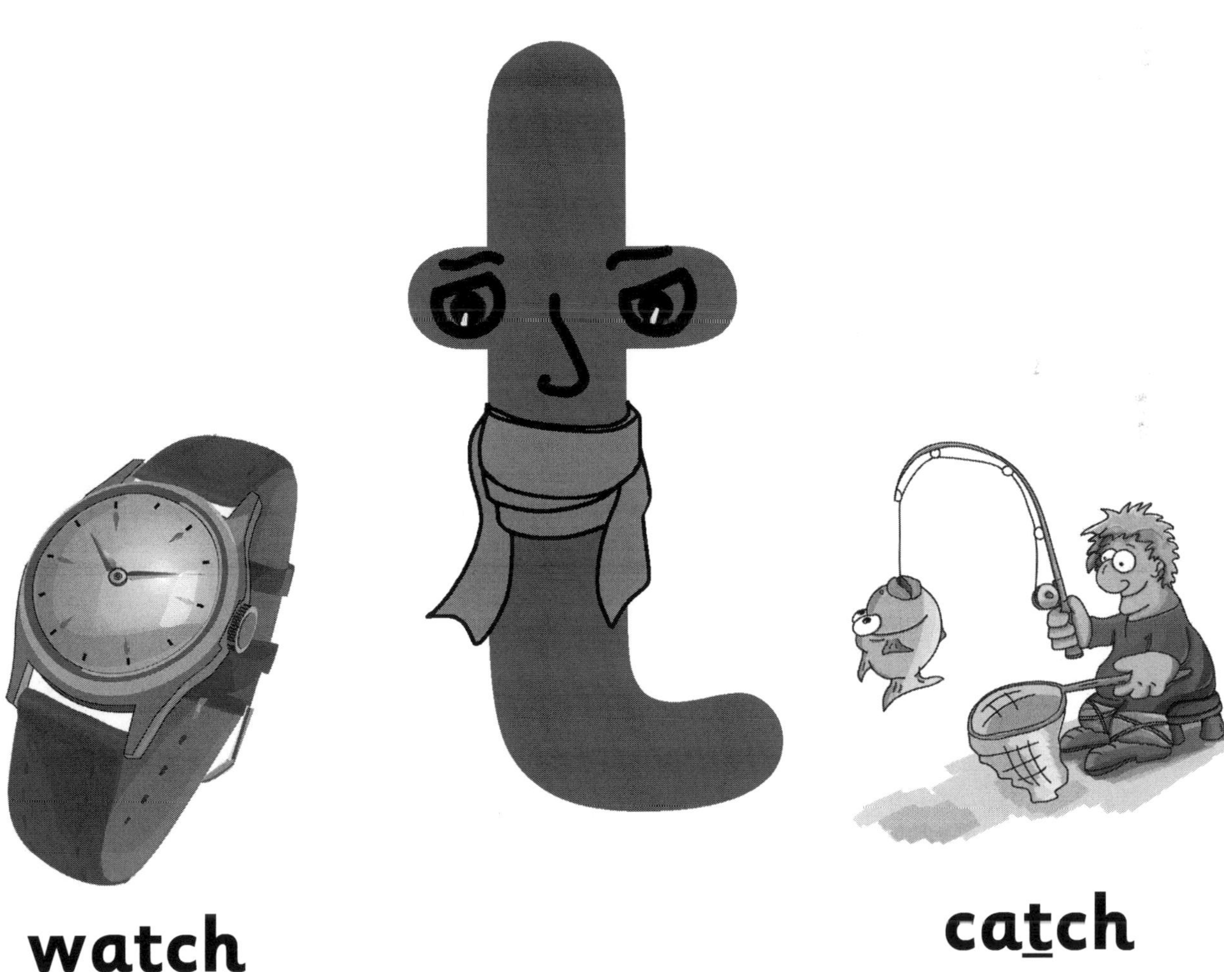

watch

catch

Police Report

One fine day in the middle of the night
two dead men got up to fight.
Back to back they faced each other,
drew their swords and shot each other.

A paralysed donkey passing by
kicked a blind man in the eye.
It knocked him through a nine-inch wall
into a dry ditch and drowned them all.

Formal vocabulary

That piece of playground rhyming is almost 200 years old! It's a classic piece of nonsense verse – and also very violent. Serious crimes are committed in the piece – fighting, shooting, assault – and three men dead!

  Cracking English Grammar in KS2 by David Horner

Now it's your turn

Your task now is to become the Police Officer, asked to write up the events in the text in a proper, formal report.

You won't alter any of the rhyme's meaning, but there must be two key features in your reporting style:

✳ First, this report has to be serious; it needs some formal vocabulary and sentences. The only long word here is *paralysed*, so you've got to change some of the original vocabulary to include more long words.

For example, two dead men can become *a pair of expired males*; *back to back* might become *facing in opposite directions but not in contact*.

Use a thesaurus for your word-searching, and use dictionary definitions to help you make your longer phrases.

✳ Second, you need to produce a report that clearly links the events of that night together into a clear narrative. People reading or listening to your report will be able to follow it better if you make it a clear sequence by linking one event to another, showing how the different bits fit together.

To do this you need some cohesive devices. These can be single words or short phrases:

eventually	as a consequence of	furthermore	then
subsequently	first of all	at the outset	at the same time

You can choose from those or any you think of yourself. Aim to add at least one cohesive device into each of the rhyme's four sentences.

Curiouser and Curiouser ...

You know how to make a noun plural – just add the suffix *-s* to the end of the noun and *cat* becomes *cat<u>s</u>*, *teacher* becomes *teacher<u>s</u>*. When a noun ends with the *s* sound we add *-es*. For example, *box* becomes *box<u>es</u>*, *wish* becomes *wish<u>es</u>*.

Irregular plurals

There's a small group of nouns which don't seem to know the rule and make their plurals in their own curious ways. Here are ten of them:

tooth/teeth	man/men	goose/geese	sheep/sheep	deer/deer
child/children	foot/feet	mouse/mice	woman/women	fish/fish

For obvious reasons, these are called irregular plurals. And now you're going to have fun with them!

Now it's your turn

You need a lined piece of paper, pencil and scissors.

* Divide your paper in half longways, either by folding or with pencil and ruler. Now, open it out.

* Down the left column, write *I saw two children*, and underneath *I saw three deer*. Write eight more lines like those, one under the other, using the numbers four to eleven followed by the rest of those awkward plural nouns from the table above – in alphabetical order.

* Now move over to the right column and start by thinking of a verb – something each of your ten nouns might do. Write each verb with the suffix *-ing* to make the present participle of each verb. For example, *I saw two children <u>talking</u>* and *I saw three deer <u>chewing</u>*.

* Finally, add an extra detail to each verb. Simple ordinary ideas are fine. Maybe, *I saw two children talking <u>in the playground</u>* and *I saw three deer chewing <u>fresh grass</u>*.

* With your scissors, cut your paper into its two halves and lay them down next to each other. Move the right half down one line. Each beginning now has a fresh – and hopefully bizarre – second half, as in this line: *I saw three deer talking in the playground*.

* Cut out the second half of your last line and put it into the gap in the top line. This now gives you ten complete lines.

* Make a final draft of your writing, with your ten lines in their new order. Show it to your friends or family, and see if they spot the ordinary lines hidden inside the very curious ones.

　　© Brilliant Publications Limited　　　　　　　Cracking English Grammar in KS2 by David Horner

Definitely NOT the Bee's Knees!

You are the toast's crusts.
You're the wasp's stings
and the test's wrong answers.

You are the storm's crashes.
You're the cat's licks
and the hay fever's sneezes.

Eva and Archie (extract)

When we really like something, we can say it is 'the cat's whiskers'. Or we might tell special friends they are 'the bee's knees'.

But what do we say to something we don't like, something that is definitely NOT the cat's whiskers? One answer is those lines by Eva and Archie.

Now it's your turn

You're going to write a poem to your very, very least favourite thing – made out of lots of other least favourite things!

✳   You just need to think of any number of not-favourite-things and make each one into a two-word phrase, like Eva and Archie did.

✳   First, think about your least favourite type of weather, job, meal, day of the week, school activity, clothes, place and so on. As many things as you can think of. Decide what is the least favourite thing about that least favourite thing, and you're ready to make your two-word phrases.

✳   To copy the form of the verses above, you need now to put your phrases into groups of three. Aim to put three quite different things into each group if you can:

   Begin each first line: *You are the* and add the two-word item.
   Begin the second line: *You're the* and add the next two-word item.
   Begin the third line: *and the* and add the third two-word item.

✳   In all three lines, there's punctuation for you to get right: The *You are* of Line 1 is shortened to *You're* in Line 2. Put an apostrophe to show the missing letter.

   Each word in each two-word phrase ends in *s*. For example, the *cat's lick<u>s</u>*. The second *s* is simply the suffix to show it's plural. But – put an apostrophe before the *s* in the first word to show there is only one owner. One cat, lots of licks!

   Be sure to do this for every not-favourite-thing in your verses – and don't forget to put the two full stops in each verse!

Forbidden Letters

It's raining, it's pouring,
the old man is snoring.
He went to bed
and bumped his head
and couldn't get up in the morning.

You probably know this one already! It's an old playground rhyme, and here's a game you might like to play with it. As well as your writing materials, you need a dice. A dictionary and a thesaurus will be useful.

You are going to rewrite that rhyme – but one letter of the alphabet is forbidden. You won't be able to use it. Here are the six forbidden letters, and to find out which one you can't use, just roll the dice. Whatever number the dice shows, that's your forbidden letter.

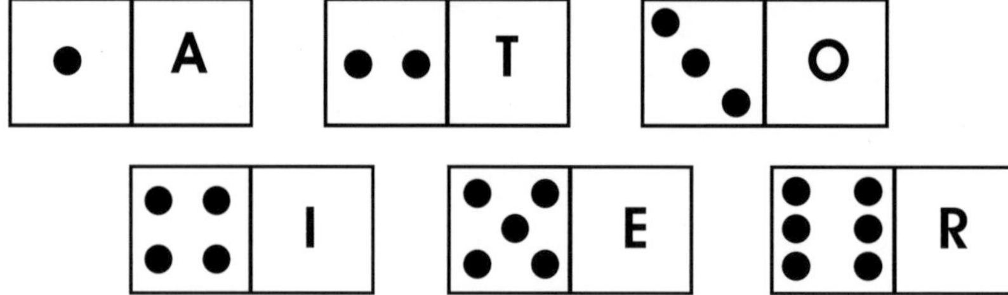

Here's a rewriting of that rhyme by Tara and Kieran, in which their forbidden letter was N:

It's wet, very wet outside,
the old chap breathes loudly as he sleeps.
He got below the duvet,
he bumped his head,
he failed to get up before midday.

Now it's your turn

This activity isn't as easy as it looks. So, here are some tips before you start:

✷   Don't try to rhyme your rewrite.

✷   Only change the bits of the rhyme that you have to, because of your forbidden letter.

✷   Be ready to hunt for synonyms and try lots of different ways to say the same thing, until you find just the right change. This will really develop your vocabulary and your sentence-making skills.

For your rewrite, you can use the rhyme at the top of the page, or one you've found yourself in a collection of nursery or playground rhymes.

        Cracking English Grammar in KS2 by David Horner

Nine Questions

Take a look at this question:

How much wood could a woodpecker peck if a woodpecker could peck wood?

The word you are going to concentrate on is *could*. This word is what is called a **modal verb**.

Modal verbs

Modal verbs go with a main verb and help to change its meaning a little. These are the ones most often used:

should	might	will	must	shall	can	could	may	would

They suggest how likely something is (*may, shall, might, will, would*); or a particular ability (*can, could*); or something necessary (*must, should*). Try them out with some main verbs to see how they work.

Now it's your turn

You are going to make some new tongue-twisting questions in the style of that original.

✳   First, choose any one of those modals – not *could* as that one's already used – to give you the key letter sound for your twister. For example, *might* will give you M.

✳   Open your dictionary at this key letter and find some words:
1.   two nouns: a thing and a living creature (human or animal). You might pick *money* and *mosquito*.
2.   one main verb: you could have *marry*.

✳   Spend time finding three words you think will make a line that's both enjoyable and a bit tricky to say out loud.

Now to start your question, using the original as your model. For example:

How much money might a mosquito marry if a mosquito might marry money?

Hint: You might need to begin your question *How many ...* , if your first noun is plural. So, for example, *How many mushrooms ...* .

Hint: Don't forget to put question marks at the end of each question!

When you're making a best draft of your own questions, put the original twister at the top. It was made up in the USA by Robert Hobart Davis back in 1902.

> If you travel to Saturn, you may
> walk round the rings for one whole day.
>
> If you land on the Moon, you must
> visit ET's BMX covered in rust.
>
> If you go to a star, you might
> find it doesn't get dark at night.
>
> Wilf and Rory (extract)

Modal verbs and clauses

Who knows where we'll be visiting a hundred years from now? Maybe our planets and beyond, as those travel tips suggest.

Look back at the rhymes and you'll see that the first lines end with a **modal verb**. These are 'helping' verbs linked to the main verb, which, in the boys' rhymes, always start the second lines. So, you don't really have to visit ET's bike, it's not an order; it's just a suggestion or a possibility.

Now it's your turn

✳ First, note down six holiday places in space, such as the Sun, a planet or an asteroid. Here are six modal verbs:

will	must	can	should	may	might

✳ Now you can write your six first lines down the page. Begin each first line *If* and then use the pattern of Wilf and Rory's first lines to help your complete your own. The rhyming lines (or 'couplets') are one complete sentence, made of two clauses. In those couplets, the subordinate clause comes first and ends at the comma, where the main clause begins.

✳ End each first line with a modal verb – and be sure you use them all.

✳ The rhymes' second lines are where you can let your imaginations loose! You'll need a rhyming word to complete each rhyme, and to save you time, here are some suggestions:

will	must	can	should	may	might
hill, chill, thrill	dust, crust, trust	man, plan, gran	mud, pud, flood	away, holiday, stay	fright, sight, height

✳ When you've chosen a rhyme-word, write it at the end of the second line and compose the rest of the line to get to that rhyme-word. It is holiday time, so be sure to make each travel tip to that place in space as exciting and inviting as you can!

Lockdown Daydreaming

> Here I am, staring out of this window,
>
> when I may have watched an England international match;
>
> when I could have gone to Liam's birthday party;
>
> when I would have had my own birthday party;
>
> when I should have been to Scotland to see granny and grandpa;
>
> when I might have enjoyed sleepovers with mates;
>
> However, here I am, staring out of this window,
>
> dreaming of the day when I shall be on that beach in Cornwall.
>
> Martyn

Spring and early summer 2020 and winter 2021 was a time when nothing happened. Nothing could happen as we locked down to keep ourselves and our families safe. In his poem, Martyn lists the things he didn't do in this period – and ends with an optimistic daydream for the future.

Now it's your turn

* Begin by noting down four or five things you didn't get to do in lockdown.

* Begin your poem, like Martyn, *Here I am*, and say where you are doing your dreaming.

  Martyn then starts the next lines with *when I* and uses five different **modal verbs** – *may, could, would, should, might* – followed by *have*.

* After each *have*, we get the main verbs. They appear as what are called **past participles**. These are made by usually (but not always) adding *-ed* to the root verb. So, as you can see, *watch* becomes *watch<u>ed</u>*, *go* becomes *gone*, etc.

  This verb form: modal + *have* + past participle is sometimes called the 'modal of lost opportunities'. It is used for events that were possible but didn't happen. In Martin's poem, you can very clearly see why it's just right. Use this verb form plus your own list of lost opportunities to make your sequence of lines.

* When you've finished the lines describing the things you've missed, add a semicolon at the end of each one.

* Now it's time to end your poem in a positive way. Use Martyn's last two lines as your model and describe something you are dreaming of doing in the future. Here, use the modal verb *shall* or *will* before your main verb to make a simple future tense. In this way, you finish on a strong, optimistic note!

Mouth Music

What is a **vowel**? We know them as *a, e, i, o, u*, but what are they really? Well, they are any sound you can make with your mouth open! Try all five and you'll see. Every other letter is a consonant, and to make any of them you need to get your tongue, teeth and lips moving!

Vowels and consonants

Here's a game all about vowels. It's usually called Obby-Dobby and when you play it you are talking (or writing) Obish. It's at least 100 years old and it's a fun way of disguising what you're talking about with friends so others can't understand you.

It's very simple; all you have to do is put the sound *ob* before every vowel or vowel sound you say or write. Ignore any 'magic e' that comes at the end of a word. So, for example:

I like you becomes *Obi lobike yobou.*

Now it's your turn

✳   First, practise by spelling and saying your name out loud in Obish. Next, try counting 1–10 in Obish. See how well and how quickly you can do these. The quicker you speak, the better you hide what you are saying!

✳   Now for consonants. This next game is really old, going at least back to Shakespeare's time and it's called Pig Latin. Nobody quite knows why, as it certainly has nothing to do with pigs!

Here's how to make Pig Latin: if a word starts with one or more consonants, just move these letters to the end of the word and add *ay*. For example:

   pig becomes *igpay*

   cheese becomes *eesechay*

   strength becomes *engthstray*

If a word starts with a vowel, spell it normally and just add *way* to the end. For example, *apple* becomes *appleway* and *under* becomes *underway*. The word *a* is simply *way*.

✳   First, practise by spelling and saying out loud some friends' names in Pig Latin. Next, try saying the days of the week in Pig Latin. Again, the clearer and quicker, the better!

✳   Finally, work with a partner to write and perform a short playscript. This can be in either Obish or Pig Latin. Or, take one 'language' each and write a short comic script, with neither of you understanding each other!

Sometimes this secret language is called Hog Latin or Dog Latin. However, in Greece, it seems, it is called the Language of Blackbirds.

    Cracking English Grammar in KS2 by David Horner

Peter Piper

Peter Piper **is picking** a peck of pickled pepper.
Did Peter Piper **pick** a peck of pickled pepper?
If Peter Piper **has picked** a peck of pickled pepper,
where **will be** the peck of pickled pepper Peter Piper **was picking**?

That has to be the best-known long tongue twister in the English language! It's at least 200–300 years old.

If you know the lines already, then you'll see we've made a few changes. We're not the first, as the original published version didn't include the adjective *pickled*.

Auxiliary verbs

The new changes are to the lines' main verbs – look at the bold words in the poem. The verbs are just a little bit longer now because, to make it even trickier to say quickly, each main verb has now got what's called an **auxiliary verb**.

Look again and you'll see them: *is*, *did*, *has*, *will* and *was*.

These are also called **helping verbs** because they 'help' the main verb to slightly change its meaning.

Now it's your turn

When you read those four lines, do you know what a peck is? It was an old unit for weighing something. Here are ten more weighing units we no longer use:

hogshead	last	wey	coomb	firkin
bushel	gill	tod	nail	stone

✳ To begin, choose any one of those units. The one you choose will give you the key initial letter for your twister. For example, bushel makes *B* your key letter.

✳ Now you're ready to write your whole four-line twister, using exactly the pattern of the original but with the nouns, main verbs and adjectives all starting with your key letter. Use a dictionary for your word hunting.

Hint: Don't forget those helpful auxiliary verbs!

Would I Lie to You?

> I have an uncle who has run the London Marathon twice.
> I used to have a rubber dinosaur that I took to bed every night.
> We owned a caravan in north Wales which blew over in a gale.
> I have a cousin whose middle name is Hector.
> I like to go to the cinema with my friends when it's my birthday.
>
> Tomos-Two-Lies

Relative pronouns and clauses

So, Tomos' answer to the question at the top is – sometimes! He's written five sentences about himself; three of them are true and two are not. Can you guess which ones are which? The answers are at the foot of this page.

Tomos had to write his sentences using a **relative pronoun** in each one. Can you spot each one? Here they are, plus one more:

who	which	whose	when	where	that

They are sometimes called the *wh-* words, plus *that*.

Each of Tomos' sentences is made of two clauses: a **main clause** at the beginning, which could be a sentence all on its own; then a **relative clause** joined to the main clause by that pronoun. For example:

I have a cousin   *whose*   *middle name is Hector.*
(main clause)   +   (relative pronoun)   +   (relative clause).

Now it's your turn

✳ Write the title, *Would I Lie to You?* at the top of your page.

✳ Underneath, write five or six sentences about yourself, some true, some not. Each sentence must be made of two clauses joined together by one of the relative pronouns.

✳ Aim to use a different **relative pronoun** in each of your sentences. This will make your writing more varied and keep your readers curious!

✳ Sign your work at the end, as Tomos did, showing how many lies readers are looking for.

Hint: As a rough guide, use *who* when writing about people; use *which* or *that* when writing about animals, places or things.

Lines 1 and 4.

 © Brilliant Publications Limited   Cracking English Grammar in KS2 by David Horner

Wise Words ...

A closed mouth catches no flies (Italy)

A spoon doesn't know the taste of soup (Wales)

No man can paddle two canoes at the same time (Central Africa)

If you go to a donkey's house, don't talk about ears (Jamaica)

A watched kettle never boils (England)

Word families and root words

Read the five proverbs from around the World. A **proverb** is a short saying, offering a truth, some advice and a bit of wisdom.

Now it's your turn

You are going to invent some brand-new proverbs of your own.

Your challenge is to make each one sound wise and meaningful, though they might not say anything sensible at all!

Look at this word: *like*.

It's what is called a **root word**. This is a word from which more words can be made, usually by adding prefixes and suffixes. The root word and all the related words are then part of a **word family**. So for our word family, the members include: *dislike, liked, unlike, liking, likely, likeable*.

Here are more root words:

happy	real	kind	play	success
comfort	behave	appear	break	care

＊   First, choose any one of those root words and make as big a word family for it as you can.

＊   Now, write your new proverb, including as many of your word family as you can. You have just one sentence and the more of the family you can cram in, the more believable your proverb becomes. So, from the *like* family we might make:

   Disliking unlikeable likes is never like liking likes.

or

   Like your unlikely likes – and your likeable likes will like you.

or

   No man can be as dislikeable as his likes can be likeable.

Twisting Time!

Thin sticks, thick bricks

Selfish shellfish

She sees cheese

Some shun sunshine

I scream, you scream, we all scream for ice-cream

A proper copper coffee pot

Word families

If you haven't tried saying those six tongue twisters, then do so immediately. Faster!

Lines like those are hard to say for two reasons; first because the words usually begin with the same or almost the same letter sound – *selfish shellfish*, for example. This is called **alliteration**.

The second reason is the sounds later in the words, for example in *I scream, you scream, we all scream for ice-cream*. Those words with that repeated *eam* letter pattern are members of what is called a **word family**.

Here are some more letter patterns you'll find in the middle and at the end of words:

ain	ight	ook	ell	ing	ail	at

Now it's your turn

You are going to write some 'word family tongue twisters'. So, first, choose a letter pattern from the ones above.

✳   Now write all the words you can think of that have this pattern. Make sure you check the spellings of your words in your dictionary.

✳   Here's an example, using the pattern, *ake*. Words might be:
snake, cake, awake, bake, take, earthquake, lake, milkshake, mistake, make, fake.

✳   Now make just some one-sentence tongue twisters, each one using just three or four of those word family words. So, with our *ake* words we might get:

Make no mistake, don't shake a snake

Let's take a lake and fake milkshakes

Awake cakes make earthquakes

    © Brilliant Publications Limited   Cracking English Grammar in KS2 by David Horner

The Great Grammar Gateau

A squelchy squirt of incredible inverted commas;
A capacious cupful of funny fronted adverbials;
A bothersome bucket of nourishing noun phrases;
A tangy tablespoon of voluptuous verbs;
One million magnificent millilitres of flatulent full stops.

Josie

The lines above are just part of a longer piece. The fun comes from it using the form of a recipe with ingredients you'd never expect to find in a cookbook!

Now it's your turn

✳ Begin by listing 8–10 different terms you know that are used to describe bits of grammar and punctuation. These terms are now your ingredients. See if you can choose your ingredients so that each one begins with a different letter of the alphabet. This will add to the variety of your work.

✳ Make a second list, this time of units of measurement used when weighing solids and liquids. You need the same number of units as you have in your ingredients list. Try again to have all your units starting with different letters.

✳ Start putting the two lists together with each unit and ingredient on a new line. These are both nouns and as you can see in the extract above, these nouns need adjectives – so be sure to leave space in each line to add these.

✳ Just as in TV baking contests, you want your recipe to be a proper showstopper. Your gateau has to look great! So, don't settle for any old adjective that comes to you – go hunting in your dictionary for unusual, unlikely ones; ones you may never have used before. You want to show off what you know about language, after all.

Hint: End each line with a semicolon – just to prove you know how to punctuate items in a list. Don't forget the full stop at the end!

Six Super Super-powers

If I were invisible,
I would cause chaos at football matches.
If I were able to speak any language,
I'd go to a new country every single day and chat to everyone I meet.
If I were able to read minds,
I would get all the test answers right.

The subjunctive

As soon as we put *If* in front of *I was*, the *was* becomes *were*. The good news is that *If I was…* is also correct. This new form is called the **subjunctive**, and we tend to use it only in very formal writing or speaking.

It's also used a lot in songs. The most famous song in the musical 'Fiddler on the Roof' is *If I were a rich man*; in 'The Wizard of Oz', the Cowardly Lion sings *If I were King of the Forest*; Beyoncé sings *If I were a boy*; and there's even a song called *If I were a Song*!

Now it's your turn

You have been granted not one, but six super-powers. However, you can only use each power once. What powers will you choose and what one thing will you do with each power?

Here are ten super super-powers for you to choose from or maybe invent your own.

to be invisible	to see through things	to be able to talk to animals	to be super strong
to be able to read minds	to be able to stay awake all the time	to be able to fly	
to be able to travel through time	to be super-clever	to be able to run very fast	

Remember, you only need to use six of them.

✳ Write your ideas as a poem. This poem will be made of six pairs of lines. The first line is the subordinate clause and the second line is the main clause. Both parts together make one sentence.

✳ For each of your chosen powers, write the first line starting, *If I were* and add the super-power. Put a comma at the end of this line.

✳ On each second line, complete the couplet by writing *I would* (or its short form *I'd*) and then say exactly what one thing you'd want to do. Put a full stop at the end of this line.

  Cracking English Grammar in KS2 by David Horner

Strange, but True

There was an old soldier from Southend-on-Sea,
<u>who</u> invited our school round for afternoon tea.

There was a long street somewhere in Carlisle,
<u>which</u> went on for mile after mile after mile.

There was an old lady in Leeds,
<u>whose</u> garden grew nothing but beautiful beads.

There was once a factory in Hull,
<u>where</u> people made motor cars out of old wool.

There was a great wizard on the Isle of Wight,
<u>that</u> knew how to make the sun rise at night.

Tara and Graeme

Relative pronouns and relative clauses

Those five comic rhymes were inspired by these opening lines to a poem by the Cornish poet, Charles Causley:

There was an old woman of Chester-Le-Street,
who chased a policeman all over his beat.

Look at those rhymes again. The two lines of each rhyme are called a **couplet**, and they make just one sentence. Each sentence is made of two **clauses**. The first line is the **main clause** – it makes sense all on its own.

The second line doesn't make complete sense on its own; it's a **relative clause**. It needs to be joined to the main clause with those little underlined words which are called **relative pronouns**.

Now it's your turn

✳   Now write your own five rhymes, telling of five strange events in five fresh places.

✳   Begin Line 1 of your five rhymes *There was* and end it with a place name. Tara and Graeme hunted in an atlas for theirs, so you can do the same.

✳   Begin Line 2 with one of the five relative pronouns – and remember you can only use each one once.

Hint: When you've written each couplet, be sure to say it out loud to check that as well as the rhyme, the lines have an even, regular rhythm.

Tall Tales

I know an old man, who is so forgetful that he leaves himself on the bus.

I once saw a pizza, which was so massive that they built a hotel on it.

I know a giraffe, which is so tall that the Man in the Moon gives it a night-night kiss.

I've walked in a fog, that was so thick that they cut it into slices and spread jam on it.

I've met a woman, who is so strong that she can squeeze a pebble like a sponge.

Extract from a group-made collection

We don't like show-offs in real life – people boasting and bragging about themselves – but we do like reading funny tall tales!

    Cracking English Grammar in KS2 by David Horner

Now it's your turn

✳   You will need two printed out copies of the cube net (page 146). One of your cubes will be for the six **nouns** in your tales, like the *old man* or the *pizza*, etc, and the other will be for the six **adjectives**, like *forgetful, massive*, etc.

   Here are six possible nouns:

| boy | girl | dragon | river | ice cream | car |

   Here are six possible adjectives:

| strange | small | noisy | dark | clever | deep |

✳   You need to choose six nouns for one cube and six adjectives for the other. Use the examples above or ones you have thought of yourself. When you have decided on your words, write your nouns, one on each face of one net and then the adjectives on the face of the other net. Then make each net into a cube.

✳   Look back at those five tall tales again. The sentences all follow the same **complex sentence** pattern. The **main clause** comes first, beginning *I…* and ending with a comma. You know it's the **main clause** each time because those words can make a whole sentence on their own.

✳   The **subordinate**, (or **relative clause**) makes the second half of each sentence, beginning with the **relative pronoun** *who, which* or *that*.

✳   Now roll your two cubes. Begin writing your one-sentence tall tale. Follow the pattern of the examples given on the previous page. After the introduction, write the noun shown on the cube and stop once you've written the adjective after *so*.

✳   Add a relative pronoun (*that, who* or *which*) and now come up with the most impossibly tall tale-ending you can think of that fits your noun and adjective.

To make more tall tales, just repeat the activity, starting with fresh noun/adjective combinations each time!

Hint: When you put in the relative pronoun each time, remember this: *who* is for humans; *which* and *that* are for animals, places or things.

What Mrs Green Saw ...

Krishnan Kipper, who flew to the moon, came back at the end of June.

Billie Bright, who went for a walk, didn't stop till she reached New York.

Jimmy Juggle, who climbed into bed, slept with his teddy on his head.

Natan Nibble, who kept a duck, read it stories from a picture book.

Mrs Green, who saw the scene, put the pictures in a magazine.

(Group-made lines)

Embedded clauses

Read these lines, looking carefully at how they are made. What do they have in common?

You'll see that every line is *one* sentence, but it's made out of *two* clauses. In each sentence, the main clause is wrapped neatly round the second clause. The second clause is put in the middle of the sentence, like a filling in a sandwich. And of course, in the lines above, the two clauses rhyme!

Clauses written like this are called **embedded clauses**, and as you can see, they are separated from the two halves of the main clause by two commas.

You can always spot a main clause, because it can make a sentence on its own, as in the line, *Jimmy Juggle slept with his teddy on his head*. The embedded clause, *who climbed into bed*, doesn't make sense by itself.

Now it's your turn

The group who made those lines used a traditional playground rhyme as their starting point. You can use their lines as your model, adding to their collection!

* Begin each line with a first name and a surname. It doesn't matter if it's not a real surname each time – just have two parts that alliterate, to get the comedy started.

* After the two names, add a comma + *who*. Next you need the embedded clause's main verb (as in *flew*, *went*, etc) and now think of your rhyming words to end each clause (as in *moon/June*, *walk/New York* etc.) Try out a few different ideas until you get a rhyming line you think works well.

* You can use the line beginning *Mrs Green* as your last line if you like. You could then make a cartoon strip of your rhymes, with pictures and your lines as captions underneath each one.

     Cracking English Grammar in KS2 by David Horner

When

When I am an adjective, I'll be <u>strange</u> in chapter six of The Girl of Ink and Stars.

I'll be on the back cover of The London Eye Mystery when I'm the adverb <u>simultaneously</u>.

When I'm a conjunction, I will be <u>but</u> at the end of The Wonders of Nature encyclopaedia.

I will be on page five of Alice in Wonderland when I'm the pronoun <u>she</u>.

When I'm a verb, I'll be <u>swept</u> at the start of The Nutcracker.

And I'll be in page six of my Frida Kahlo book when I'm the noun <u>blouses</u>.

Elizabeth

Main clauses and subordinate clauses

Each of these six sentences is made up of two parts. These parts are called clauses. There's a **main clause** and a **subordinate clause**. It's very easy to see which is which. The main clause makes perfect sense by itself. So, for example, *I will be on page five of Alice in Wonderland*, could be a sentence all on its own. But *when I'm a pronoun* on its own doesn't feel complete; it needs a main clause to join on to.

To keep her writing interesting, Elizabeth keeps swapping the order of the two clauses round. Look again and you'll see that in Lines 1, 3 and 5, the subordinate clause comes first but in Lines 2, 4 and 6, the main clause comes first.

Finally, Elizabeth shows us she knows her word classes and, most importantly, tells us her current favourite books!

Now it's your turn

✳ First, write down your own favourite book titles. No more than seven!

Here are the seven most common word classes:

noun	adjective	verb	adverb	preposition	conjunction	pronoun

✳ Note down the ones you recognise and write each of them once beside each of your book titles.

✳ Now look in your chosen books for an example of the part of speech and note that down too.

✳ You are ready now to compose your lines in the same way Elizabeth did. Like her, start your last line with *And* to show your list is ending.

Hint: When you write your lines, don't forget that when the subordinate clause comes first, you need a comma at the end of it. Remember, you don't need a comma when the main clause comes first. Just like in these two sentences!

Words of Warning

> Never set sail until Sunday is over.
>
> Take care not to wind wool while you are working by lamplight.
>
> Do not mention or talk about hares or pigs whenever you are baiting a line.
>
> On no account leave harbour unless you are wearing a navy-blue jumper knitted by your mother or your wife.

Subordinating conjunctions

It seems that fishermen, like lots of footballers, are a bit superstitious! These four superstitions were collected in the village of Flamborough on the North-East coast of England.

Are you superstitious? Do you cross your fingers, touch wood, never walk under ladders or fear the number 13? If the answer to any of these is 'yes', then you are!

Now it's your turn

✳ Now it's time to invent some brand-new superstitions. Those Flamborough superstitions were intriguing because they were quite complicated, and yours are going to be just the same!

✳ Each of those superstitions is just one sentence long, but made of two halves. Each half starts with a **main clause**, (which can make sense on its own), and ends with a **subordinate clause**, and the two clauses are joined together by a **subordinating conjunction**. The conjunctions are: *until*, *while*, *whenever* and *unless*.

Here are some more:

when	after	before	once	wherever	if

✳ To make your own superstitions always use the pattern:

main clause + conjunction + subordinate clause.

Above all, make each one as wacky and entertaining as you can!

    Cracking English Grammar in KS2 by David Horner

All The Ones They Call Lowly

Garter snake, garter snake, you hurt no one;
You move on so gracefully through the grass.
Garter snake, garter snake, I'll be your friend
And not run away as you pass.

Grasshopper, grasshopper, hopping so high
Away from our crazy feet close to you;
Grasshopper, grasshopper, I'll be your friend;
I wish I could hop as high as you.

Speckled frog, speckled frog, I like your pad;
I don't believe I'll catch warts from you.
Speckled frog, speckled frog, I'll be your friend;
Why should I be frightened of you?

Wriggly worm, wriggly worm, get back inside –
A robin is waiting to take you home;
Wriggly worm, wriggly worm, I'll be your friend;
Above ground you'll not be alone.

All the ones that they do call lowly,
That do no harm to you or me –
Each will be my secret buddy
On grass and water, sand and tree.

David Campbell

Second person

David Campbell was born and grew up in Guyana in South America. As well as writing poetry, he was a painter, singer and song writer!

In his poem, 'All The Ones They Call Lowly', he speaks straight to the four animals, calling each one *you* and *your*. This is called writing in the **second person**. He also writes to them in the present tense, so it feels as if each creature is right in front of him

The word 'lowly' means ordinary, everyday or unimportant. David chooses creatures to write to which are found all over Guyana. And in choosing them, he at once makes each one matter and become important.

Now it's your turn

You need your own 'lowly' creatures to write to. Hedgehog? Sparrow? Ladybird? You choose.

Use the simple pattern of David's poem as your model. Here are some details to get you started:

✳ Each verse is just four lines.

✳ In Lines 1 and 3, name your chosen creature twice.

✳ Line 3 always ends: *I'll be your friend.*

✳ Lines 2 and 4 rhyme, sometimes just by repeating the word *you*. You can do the same or have no rhyme at all in your poem.

✳ In each verse tell the animal a few things you know and feel about it.

✳ In his last verse, he uses the second person, but this time the *you* becomes all the readers of the poem. You can have this verse as your ending or write your own if you wish.

     Cracking English Grammar in KS2 by David Horner

It Can't Play Itself, You Know!

The Trombone Speaks Out

Sometimes I am left in my case, having a break from all the noise. But on other days I am played so loudly, as my slide is moved back and forth. I am blown into with such an almighty force, that I am deafened for a while. Sometimes I get filled with spit, so I start to gargle until I am emptied out. My shiny coat gets dented as I am whacked into the stand. After half an hour I will be put back in my box, waiting to serve my purpose again.

Aidan

We humans are always doing things. We can't stop. We are made to be active. However, musical instruments, like that trombone, can't do anything for themselves. They need us to play them! They are therefore **passive**.

The passive voice

If you look back at Aidan's talking trombone, you can see clearly that it gets things done to it. It's the verbs in the writing that make this clear. If Aidan was describing playing his trombone, he would say what he does, with verbs in what is called the **active voice**. However, the trombone's verbs are passive, using the **passive voice**. How many examples of the passive voice can you spot in the trombone's speech?

Now it's your turn

✳   First, choose a musical instrument: one that you blow into, or you strum, or you press with your fingers or you stroke with a bow; or maybe you even hit!

✳   Think hard about your instrument, so hard that you can imagine being that instrument! When you are ready, jot down all the different things that you have done to you. If you look up your first passive verb in your thesaurus, you'll have some useful synonyms to work with.

✳   You must decide for yourself if your instrument likes and enjoys its passive life!

Hint: Don't say how your instrument feels about its life. All the passive verbs mean your readers will be able to sense the instrument's life for themselves.

You Are What You Do

> Hello everyone. I <u>am</u> Joshua.
> I like <u>building</u> sandcastles on the beach.
> My hobby is <u>collecting</u> football cards.
> I don't like <u>dancing</u> at school.
> I love <u>eating</u> mint choc chip ice cream.
> I <u>feel</u> good when I have <u>finished</u> all my homework.
>
> (extract)

The active voice

We are all, every one of us, what we do. Because we are living creatures, we are born to be active, to do things – even when we are asleep! In Joshua's lines, he is building up an A-Z (or **abecedarius**) of 26 of his activities with the verbs appearing in alphabetical order.

In the extract all the verbs have been highlighted. Verbs have two forms (or voices): either **active** or **passive**. So, when you throw a ball, you are doing something, you are active, and the verb is also in the **active voice**. When your teeth are being checked, you are passive, you are having something done to you, and the verb is now in the **passive voice**.

So your abecedarius will have, 26 lines all together. And as it is all about activities, it's only right that all your verbs are in the **active voice**.

Now it's your turn

✳   In your own autobiographical A–Z, every line will describe an activity of yours – things you do now; things you have done in the past; things you want to do in the future; things you like doing and things you don't like doing; things you are proud of having done.

✳   Each line should take no more than one line of your page, with those 26 verbs in order.

✳   To get started, make notes or a rough draft. Write the alphabet down the side of a page and note down ideas, with the all-important verb, as they come to you. Don't try to work in alphabetical order – that is for later when you make your final draft.

✳   Joshua began with a greeting and his name as an introduction. You can do the same if you like. Looking through your dictionary can often help you get ideas for your verbs – and don't panic when you get to *x*; just use *ex* instead.

      Cracking English Grammar in KS2 by David Horner

Witches' Brew

Double, double toil and trouble;
Fire burn, and cauldron bubble.
    Frogs' feathers and wellies' wings,
    birds' beards and snakes' songs,
    elephants' eggs and clouds' coats,
    snowballs' socks and teapots' tongues,
    trees' tummies and lampposts' legs.
Double, double toil and trouble;
Fire burn, and cauldron bubble.

Apostrophes

In William Shakespeare's play 'Macbeth', a scene begins with the stage directions:

In a dark cave. In the middle, a cauldron bubbling. Thunder. Enter the three Witches.

The witches begin their spell-making by chanting the two lines that open and end that piece at the top of the page. The rest, the actual ingredients to go into the bubbling cauldron, was co-written by Isaac, Amira and Luke.

Now it's your turn

If you can, work with one or two partners to write and then perform your piece together.

✳ First, look back at the spell and read it out loud – more than once, if you can. See what you notice about the patterns of the lines as you do.

✳ Notice how each line of the witches' chant has two ingredients for the cauldron, linked by the **conjunction** *and* – and each ingredient is completely impossible!

Every ingredient is made of two words – two **nouns** to make a **noun phrase**. Both the nouns end in *s*, don't they? That's because both nouns are plurals – lots of frogs and lots of feathers!

However, the first *s* has an **apostrophe** after it and the second one doesn't. This is because, if frogs could have feathers, they would own (or possess) them. That apostrophe shows this ownership and goes after the plural *s*.

The last *s* on the word *feathers* is simply to show that it is a plural noun with no apostrophe needed. Look back and you'll see the same pattern in all the chant's ingredients.

✳ Now make your own ingredients to include in your witches' (or wizards') chant. Each one has to alliterate (*wellies' wings, clouds' coats*) and be as impossibly strange as you can make it. Aim to make at least five pairs of ingredients and add the rhyme from 'Macbeth' at the top and bottom to frame your own lines.

✳ Writing finished, it's time to get into character!
Rehearse and perform your whole chant –
and have fun!

    Cracking English Grammar in KS2 by David Horner

Writing Painting

Berwick-Upon-Tweed L. S. Lowry

A girl.
A thin girl.
A thin, staring girl.

That pub.
That grey pub.
That grey, closed pub.

One lamppost.
One wobbly lamppost.
One bent, wobbly lamppost.

Nina

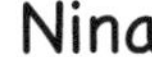

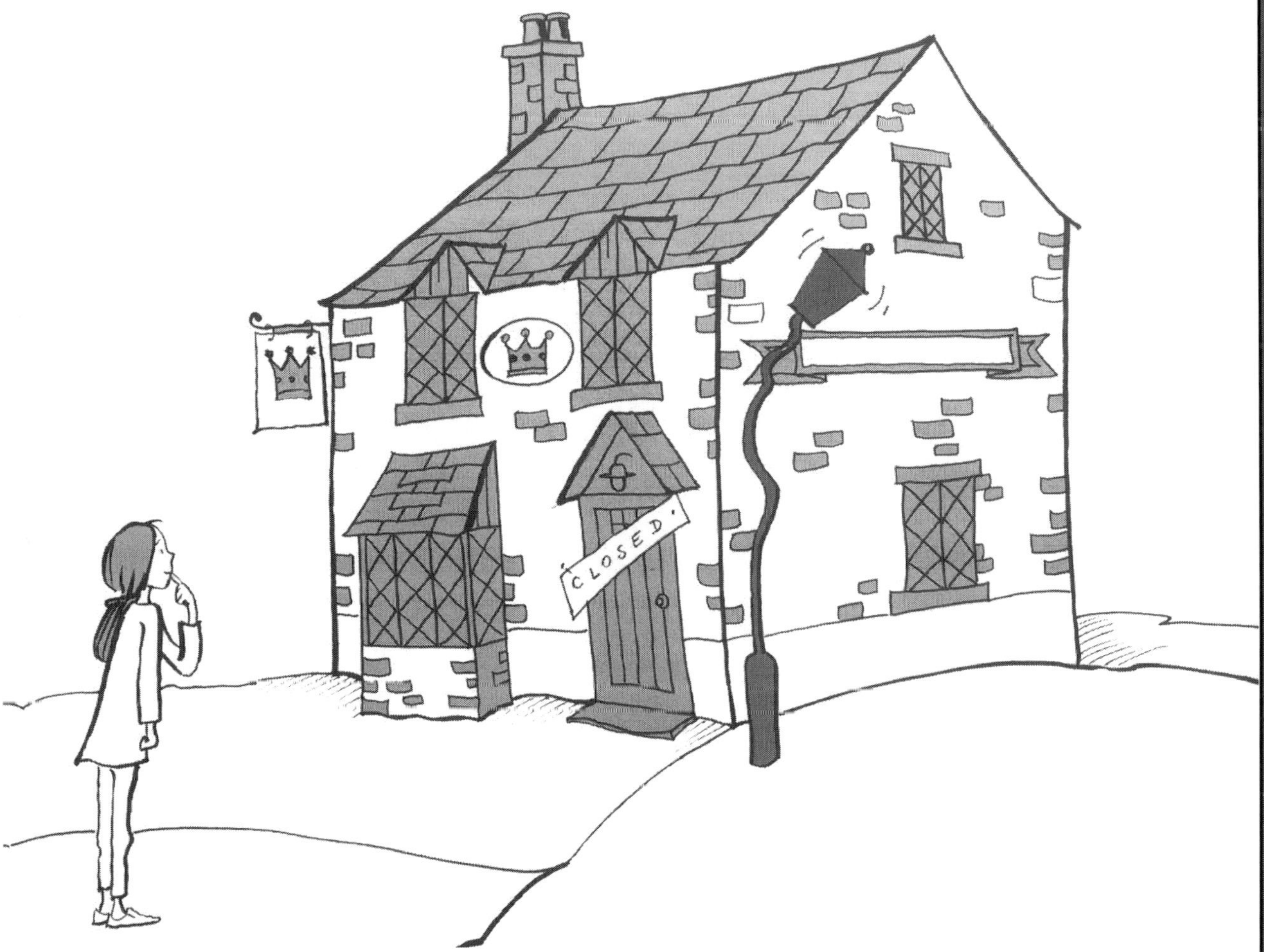

Expanded noun phrases and determiners

If you are telling an exciting story, then you want to hurry the reader along, and you use verbs to do this. Verbs are all about action, to show that things are happening.

Adjectives, on the other hand, slow things down, and there are times when this is what the writer wants. An example is Nina's writing, based on a painting by L. S. Lowry. She wants you to read slowly and carefully, just like she did with the actual painting. The repetition and the steady build-up of each line emphasises every detail and captures our curiosity. All done with not a single verb!

Now it's your turn

✳ Choose a picture – it can be a painting or a photograph.

✳ Spend time studying your picture; wander all around it and really get to know it.

✳ Pick out three details you have noticed and on a scrap of paper note each one down in any order. This will give you three **nouns**.

✳ Keep looking back at the picture and for each noun add an **adjective**.

✳ Now add a second adjective to each noun – one that says something different about the noun. For example, Nina wouldn't choose synonyms like *skinny, slim, bony* after *thin*. Your second adjective must bring something new; it must do some work and earn its place.

✳ You now have three **expanded noun phrases** – and to finish things off, each one needs an introductory word. Nina used *A, That* and *One*. Words like these are called **determiners** – they introduce nouns and always come before them. There are lots of different ones. Any number is a determiner, as are these words:

this	the	these	those
her	his	their	your
some	a few	many	several

✳ Choose three different determiners from these (and Nina's) to introduce your noun phrases.

✳ Write your final draft. Put the name of your picture and artist as your title. To slow the reader down even more, set each group of phrases on your page as a poem in lines, one under the other, like Nina did:

> A girl.
> A thin girl.
> A thin, staring girl

Dictionary Corner

The Cruise of the 'P.C.'

Across the swiffling waves they went,
The gumly bark yoked to and fro:
The jupple crew on pleasure bent,
Galored, "This is a go!"

Beside the poo's'l stood the Gom,
He chirked and murgled in his glee;
While near him, in a grue jipon,
The Bard was quite at sea.

"Gollop! Golloy! Thou scrumjous Bard!
Take pen (thy stylo) and endite
A pome, my brain needs kurgling hard,
And I will feast tonight."

That wansome Bard he took his pen,
A flirgly look around he guv;
He squoffled once, he squirled, and then
He wrote what's writ above.

Anonymous

The Cruise of the 'P.C.' first appeared in a book published in America back in 1903 and we have no idea who wrote it.

It might have been written as a nonsense poem, or it might just be a very old poem – or *pome* as the poet spells it – full of words we no longer use or even understand!

This is where you come in. You are going to become a dictionary-maker, a lexicographer (we say it lex-i-cog-raph-er). Don't panic – you're not going to write the whole dictionary, just a **glossary** – a list in alphabetical order – of the lost words used in the poem. There are 4–5 such words in each verse and they are almost all **nouns**, **verbs** or **adjectives**.

In your glossary as in all dictionaries, each entry needs three things:
1. the word – called the head word – in bold print, or in colour
2. what part of speech each word is. This appears in italics or brackets
3. a short, clear explanation of the word's meaning

To help you, here are two words as they will appear in your glossary.
bard *noun* a poet who writes poems to celebrate brave deeds.
bark *noun* a large 3-masted sailing ship, dating back to the 17th century.

Now it's your turn

You will need a dictionary and perhaps a partner to work with.

✳   On your copy of the poem, underline all the words in each verse that you don't recognise. Check to see if they are in your dictionary. If they are not there, then write down the word for your glossary.

✳   Read each verse carefully to help you work out what part of speech each word is, and what you think it could mean. What are *swiffling* waves like? What was the boat doing when it *yoked*? What is a *jupple* crew? And who or what is the *Gom*?

✳   Always remember, you can't be wrong about any word in this activity! All it needs is your best guess every time. Here are some talking points for some of the words in each verse:

    Verse 1 *swiffling* – the suffix *-ing* tells us that this is an adjective made from a verb. So what might the verb be?

    Verse 2 *poo's'l* – the apostrophes show us that there are letters missing. What letters can you suggest to complete the word?

    Verse 3 *Gollop! Golloy!* – these two words are followed by exclamation marks. How would you say the two words? What mood do they suggest to you?

    Verse 4 *guv* – look at where the word appears and the surrounding sentences. Could it be the past tense of a verb? What do you think the verb might be?

✳   When you have worked on all your words (about 20 all together) write them out in your glossary. Don't forget they have to be in alphabetical order!

        Cracking English Grammar in KS2 by David Horner

Group Game 1: Our Classroom Rules

First, form a group of 3–6 players. Everyone needs a pen or pencil and their own copy of the Game Grid (page 142), and a dictionary each.

Turn your grid landscape way round, so you have a table with five columns and four rows.

Choose someone to read out the instructions below. Don't look at what other people write, as this will spoil the fun of the Great Reveal at the end!

Instructions

You will always write down one column, filling in the four boxes of the column each time. Listen carefully and don't rush.

Column 1: Write four different **adjectives**, one in each of the boxes in this column. You can find these in a dictionary. The dictionary will also tell you if a word is an adjective, maybe using *adj.* for short. Begin each adjective with a **capital letter** and after each adjective, add a **comma**.

When everyone has filled Column 1, fold the paper over to hide the writing underneath. Everyone passes their grid to the left – no peeping!

Column 2: In each box, write a different colour. Then fold the paper over to hide the writing underneath. Everyone passes their grid to the left.

Column 3: In each box, write something you will find in your classroom (four nouns). Make each noun plural by adding *s* to the end of each one. When everyone has done this, fold the paper over to hide the writing underneath. Everyone passes their grid to the left.

Column 4: Here are four **auxiliary** (helping) **verbs**: *can't, won't, don't, mustn't.* Write each of these words into the four boxes, in any order you like. Make sure you put the apostrophes in the right places. Now add a **main verb** after each auxiliary verb. You can find these verbs in your dictionary, where they may be marked just with a *v.* When everyone has done this, fold the paper over to hide the writing underneath. Everyone passes their grid to the left.

Column 5: Write four more **adjectives**, one in each box. Use your dictionaries to find unusual ones! Make the adjectives into **adverbs** by adding *ly* to the end of each one. Finally, put a full stop after each adverb.

Time for the Big Reveal! Each player unfolds their grid and reads out their four sentences.

Check everyone's writing has four capital letters, four commas, four apostrophes and four full stops.

You have now shown that you can use **commas to separate items in a list**; you can write an **expanded noun phrase** (two adjectives and a noun); you can put **apostrophes into words to show missing letters**; you can **change adjectives into adverbs**.

Group Game 2: Four Warnings!

First, form a group of 3–6 players. Everyone needs a pen or pencil and their own copy of the Game Grid (page 142), along with a dictionary and a thesaurus each.

Turn your grid landscape way round, with five columns and four rows. Choose someone to read out the instructions below. Don't look at what other people write, as this will spoil the fun of the Big Reveal at the end!

Instructions

You will always write down one column, filling in the four boxes of the column each time. Listen carefully and don't rush. And no peeping!

Column 1: Write *Never*, starting with a **capital letter**, in each box in this column. After each Never, write a verb that means *move*. You need four different **verbs**, so use your thesaurus.

When everyone has filled Column 1, fold the paper over to hide the writing underneath. Everyone passes their grid to the left.

Column 2: In each box write a different wild animal. Put with *a* or with *an* correctly before each animal. When everyone has done this, fold the paper over to hide the writing. Everyone passes their grid to the left.

Column 3: Write the **adverb** *when* in each box. Here are four **noun prefixes**: *super, anti, hyper, mega*. Write one in each box in any order you like. Add a family relation to each **prefix**, for example, *brother, granny*. When everyone is ready, fold the paper over to hide the writing and pass the grids to the left.

Column 4: In each box write the **auxiliary** (helping) **verb** *has*. After each *has*, add a **main verb** that means *cook*. Look in your thesaurus again. Make each main verb into its **past participle** – usually by adding *ed* or just *d* to the end. So, *cook* becomes *cook<u>ed</u>, bake* becomes *bake<u>d</u>*. Your dictionary might help you here. When everyone is ready, fold the paper over to hide the writing and pass the grids to the left.

Column 5: Write a different item of clothing in each of the four boxes. Before each one, write *a* or *an* correctly. After each bit of clothing, add a full stop.

Time for the Big Reveal! Each player unfolds their grid and reads out their four sentences.

Check everyone's writing has four capital letters, and four full stops. Finally, look at those little words in boxes 2 and 5: check that you have all used *a* (before a consonant) or *an* (before a vowel) correctly.

You have now shown that you can use **adverbs and conjunctions of time in a sentence**; you can make **nouns using prefixes**; you can use **the correct form of *a* or *an* before the next word**; you can form the **present perfect tense of a verb**.

    Cracking English Grammar in KS2 by David Horner

Group Game 3: A Look into the Future!

First, form a group of 3–6 players. Everyone needs a pen or pencil and their own copy of the Game Grid (page 142), along with a dictionary and a thesaurus each.

Turn your grid landscape way round, with five columns and four rows.

Choose someone to read out the instructions below. Don't look at what other people write, as this will spoil the fun of the Big Reveal at the end!

Instructions

You will always write down one column, filling in the four boxes of the column each time. Listen carefully and don't rush.

Column 1: Here are four **adverbs**: *Before, After, At, By*. Use each of them once to write into your four boxes, starting each one with a **capital letter**. After each **adverb**, add a different time: an exact time of day, a day of the week, a season, a special day of the year. Put a **comma** after each time.

When everyone has filled Column 1, fold the paper over to hide the writing underneath. Everyone passes their paper to the left. No peeping!

Column 2: Write the names of four of your friends – one in each box. After each name, add '*s*, (*apostrophe s*). Write the word *pet* after each name. When everyone has done this, fold the paper over to hide the writing underneath. Everyone passes their paper to the left.

Column 3: Write four different wild animals – one in each box. When everyone has done this, fold the paper over to hide the writing underneath. Everyone passes their paper to the left.

Column 4: Write the phrase *will have* in each box. After each phrase, add a **main verb** that means *clean*. Look in your thesaurus for your words. Add *ed* or *d* to the end of each **main verb**. For example, *wash* becomes *will have washed* and *wipe* becomes *will have wiped*. This is called the **future perfect tense**. When everyone has done this, fold the paper over to hide the writing underneath. Everyone passes their paper to the left.

Column 5: Write any number between 2 and 10 in each box. Write a different musical instrument after each number, adding *s* to each one to make them plural.

Time for the Big Reveal! Each player unfolds their grid and reads out their four sentences.

Check everyone's writing has four capital letters, four commas, four apostrophes before four plural musical instruments ending in *s* and four full stops.

You have now shown that you can **write a fronted adverbial with a comma after**; **use an apostrophe to show the difference between plural and possessive** *s*; **use a Standard English tense: the future perfect.**

Group Game 4: Noisy Neighbours

First, form a group of 3–6 players. Everyone needs a pen or pencil and their own copy of the Game Grid (page 142), and a dictionary each.

Turn your grid landscape way round, with five columns and four rows.

Choose someone to read out the instructions below. Don't look at what other people write, as this will spoil the fun of the Big Reveal at the end!

Instructions

You will always write down one column, filling in the four boxes of the column each time. Listen carefully. Don't rush, and no peeping!

Column 1: Here are four **adverbs**: *Possibly, Surely, Perhaps, Maybe*. Write a different one in each box, starting each with a **capital letter**. Think of four different animals that can fly and write one after each adverb. Between the adverb and the animal add *a* (before a **consonant**) or *an* (before a **vowel**). Put a **comma** after each animal.

When everyone has filled Column 1, fold the paper over to hide the writing underneath. Everyone passes their grid to the left.

Column 2: Write the **relative pronoun** *which* to begin and then in each box add a **main verb** that means *makes a noise.* Use your thesaurus here. Remember to add an *s* to the end of each verb. When everyone is ready, fold the paper over to hide the writing underneath. Everyone passes their grid to the left.

Column 3: Write the preposition *inside* and then after each one any container – from an egg cup to a barrel in size. Before each one add *a* or *an* correctly. Put a **comma** after each container. When everyone is ready, fold the paper over to hide the writing underneath. Everyone passes their grid to the left.

Column 4: Here are four **modal verbs**: *could, would, might, should*. Write a different one into each box. Add any **verb** which means *move*. Use your thesaurus again to help you. When everyone is ready, fold the paper over to hide the writing underneath. Everyone passes their grid to the left.

Column 5: Write the **preposition** *to* in each box and then add the name of any country in the world – starting each one with a **capital letter**. Finish with a full stop.

Time for the Big Reveal! Each player unfolds their grid and reads out their four sentences.

Check everyone's writing has eight capital letters and four full stops.

You have now shown that you can show possibility **using adverbs and modal verbs**; introduce a **relative clause in a sentence**; use **capital letters to start proper nouns**.

     Cracking English Grammar in KS2 by David Horner

Group Game 5: Scenes from our Scary Movie

First, form a group of 3–6 players. Everyone needs a pen or pencil and their own copy of the Game Grid (page 142), along with a dictionary each.

Turn your grid landscape way round, with five columns and four rows.

Choose someone to read out the instructions below. Don't look at what other people write, as this will spoil the fun of the Big Reveal at the end!

Instructions

You will always write down one column, filling in the four boxes of the column each time. Listen carefully and don't rush. Use your thesaurus to help your word searching in Columns 1, 3 and 5.

First of all, at the top of the grid, everyone writes, *In our scary movie we have:* And don't forget the colon.

Column 1: Put four bullet points to start each box. After each bullet, write *the*. Add four different **adjectives** meaning *beautiful*, one adjective in each box.

When everyone has filled Column 1, fold the paper over to hide the writing underneath. Everyone passes their grid to the left. No peeping!

Column 2: Write four different, large buildings, one into each box. When everyone has done this, fold the paper over to hide the writing underneath. Everyone passes their grid to the left.

Column 3: Write *is*. Now add any **main verb** that means *eat*. This verb must be in the **passive voice**, so, for example, *eat* becomes *eaten*, *swallow* becomes *swallowed*. When everyone has done this, fold the paper over to hide the writing underneath. Everyone passes their grid to the left.

Column 4: Write *by the*. Add four different **adjectives** meaning *ugly*, one adjective in each box. When everyone has done this, fold the paper over to hide the writing underneath. Everyone passes their grid to the left.

Column 5: Write a different minibeast into each box. Put a **semicolon** after the first three minibeasts and a **full stop** after the third.

Time for the Big Reveal! Each player unfolds their grid and reads the introduction and the four movie scenes.

You have now shown that you can **use the colon, bullet points and semicolons; write verbs in the passive voice; use a range of adjectival synonyms and antonyms**.

If you are going to be a secret agent, you must be able to keep secrets! You must also know who you can trust and how to pass secret messages on to them.

Here is a message given to an agent in the past:

```
February eighth –
Remember to meet Ms Z
Under the library clock. She is
Important
To our mission.
```

Easy enough to read, but have you spotted something else? Look at the letters at the start of each line. See, they spell FRUIT. The message itself doesn't matter; it's just meant to confuse other people who might read it. Those letters spell a code-word, one that our agent had to receive.

We keep lots of such code-words. They are hidden away on spelling lists used in schools in Years 3–4 and 5–6 (see pages 143–144). These youngsters and their teachers never suspect that really, these lists come from MI5.

Have a copy of the spelling list for Y3–4 handy and look at that message one more time. Can you find other words in both the list and the message? That's right, *February*, *eighth*, *remember*, *library*. Agents know they can trust the code-word if the message includes more words from the list.

Here's another example. The code-word here comes from the Y5–6 list. Have it by you to spot more words from it.

```
You will recognise
Agent Forty. You
Cannot trust
Her.
Thorough care needed!
```

Code-word: *YACHT*; extra list-words: *recognise*, *forty* and *thorough*.

A message made like this, where the initial letters of each line spell a word, is called an **acrostic**.

Now, as part of your training, choose a word yourself from your list and write an **acrostic** for it. Include at least two extra words from your list to prove the message is genuine – and **no spelling mistakes!**

First, a message for you:

```
Now you are back,
you need to pose as a penguin
keeper at the city zoo.
You must therefore learn how
to fill
their special pool each day before
leaving. Your contact wears a favourite red
scarf and will be riding
an ordinary bicycle.
```

But what exactly is the message? Is it what it says? Or is it a message with a secret meaning – an acrostic, perhaps, with the letters starting each line spelling a word? Well it's neither of these. But there is a secret message!

Don't look at the letters starting each line, but at the ones ending the lines. Write them down if you like and you'll find they spell the word KNOWLEDGE. The message is meant only to disguise this key word.

This kind of writing is called a **telestich**. It comes from the Greek word *telos*, meaning 'end'. We use an **acrostic** for a secret message and a **telestich** for a TOP secret one. As you may know, we keep our code-words stored on school spelling lists.

This one comes from the Year 3–4 list (see pages 143) and we've added other words from that list so the agent receiving the message will know it is genuine. Six words in all – *learn, therefore, special, favourite, ordinary, bicycle*.

Here is another telestich message. The code-word here comes from the Y5–6 list (see page 144) with more list words hidden inside.

```
This is
an important message:
according to a BBC
reporter
there is a microphone
spotted in a foreign restaurant
hidden in a variety of pasta.
You must go over
to check immediately.
```

Code-word: *SECRETARY* plus *according, foreign, restaurant, variety* and *immediately*.

Now as part of your training, choose a word from your list and write a telestich for it. Include at least two words – more if you can – from your list to prove the message is genuine – and most importantly – no spelling mistakes!

Welcome to Spy School: Task 3

Here are the ingredients for a recipe you might like to try:

1/5 of a grapefruit
1/6 of early apples
1/7 ounce of mustard
1/3 jar of a certain marmalade

Does it look okay to you? Or not quite right? If you are a bit suspicious, then you might have what it takes to become a special agent, trusted to send and receive secret messages.

It isn't a real recipe, but it does have hidden inside it one important key word.

Here's how to find it: each ingredient starts with one or more of the letters that spell out the key word. So:

- grapefruit has 10 letters. If you write down the first two of them – and therefore 1/5 of the whole word – you get *GR*.

- apples has six letters, the first being A - so now we have *GRA*

- 1/7 of mustard gives *M* and 1/3 of marmalade is *MAR*.

- So, the keyword is *GRAMMAR*

Only the fraction and the ingredient matter. These give the clues to the key word the agent must receive. The rest is just detail, meant to hide the recipe's real purpose. Here at MI5, we have many such words, all kept safe on school spelling lists (see pages 143–144), where no one will suspect anything! So our agents can trust the messages they get, we always try to include more words from the lists – in the recipe above, the words are *early* and *certain* from the Y3–4 set.

Here's another recipe, this time from the Y5–6 list:

3/7 of a bunch of parsley
1/4 of a lime
1/5 gram of icing
1/7 of any available apricot
2/5 of melon
1/6 nutmeg
1/7 tin of treacle – nice, but not necessary

Keyword: *PARLIAMENT*; extra list-words: *available, necessary*

Now, as part of your training, choose one word from your list and write a recipe for it. Include at least two extra words from your list to prove the message is genuine – and no spelling mistakes!

Welcome to Spy School: Task 4

Read this message very carefully:

Laughing elephants never get the hiccups.

Now read it again – and remember it. And as long as you do, you will always be able to spell the word **LENGTH**. Can you work out why? That's right, the initial letters of each word in the message spell it out.

This is called a **mnemonic**: a tool to help us remember facts, information or sequences.

You probably know some already. Here's one to help you remember the colours of the rainbow:

Richard Of York Gave Battle In Vain.

So – red, orange, yellow, green, blue, indigo, violet.

Or this one for the planets:

My Very Easy Method Just Speeds Up Naming.

This helps us list the planets coming away from the Sun. Try it and see.

Here at MI5 we like **mnemonics**. (You say it nem-on-ik, by the way; the m is silent.) And we also like having lots of our key words buried away in your school spelling lists (see pages 143–144).

Here are two spelling **mnemonics**, one from the Y3–4 list and one from the Y5–6 list:

Try hopping over rainbows or under green hedges

Clever owls never sing carols in early November, causing excitement

Quickly jot the highlighted letters down in each message to find the two words.

Now choose any one word from your own spelling list to make a one-line mnemonic for it. It can be just one sentence or more. Why not choose a word you find hard to spell yourself? Make the mnemonic as daft as you like – it all helps make it memorable.

As an agent, you will need to spot and create secret messages. This task will develop your message writing skills – and improve your spelling at the same time!

To finish, here are three mnemonics by Hermione:

<u>Rhyme</u>: revision helps you memorise events

<u>Foreign</u>: five orangutans read everything in German newspapers

<u>Medicine</u>: my ears do interesting capers in nauseating exhibitions

Welcome to Spy School: Task 5

Here at MI5, we never want information to fall into the wrong hands. However, things can go wrong. It is vital therefore that if the 'wrong hands' do get hold of our messages, they do not understand what the message really means.

We keep many secret code-words, sending details and orders to our agents. These words are hidden in school spelling list (see pages 143–144), where no-one would think to look. This next exercise will give you some good practice in message-hiding. Here is an example for you to study – with a secret word included. But which word is it?

No arm upon green horses teapots yummiest.

Someone could waste a lot of time trying to work out the meaning of that. But the secret message isn't any of those words – it is the word *naughty*, spelled by the first letters of each word. It's an **acrostic sentence**. And each word of the sentence is exactly one letter longer than the one before. Read it again to see.

That word came from the Y3–4 list. Here's another one for you, this time from the Y5–6 list, and now made into two sentences, just so it looks like it might mean something. It should take you only a second or two now to find the key word.

Moon under school clothes. Lettuces expensive.

You are going to make it even trickier for those 'wrong hands' to solve.

First, choose your 'secret code-word' from your spelling list and write that word vertically down your page.

Write a word starting with the first letter of your code-word. Keep this first word really short as, remember, each word that follows must be one letter longer. Any words of the right length will do the job here. Use your dictionary for your word-hunting. Add punctuation as you wish. The stranger the false message, the better!

For your final draft, set your chosen words out in triangle or Christmas Tree form – to make the writing attractive, and finding the secret code-word even harder!

<table>
<tr><td>No</td><td>Moon</td></tr>
<tr><td>arm</td><td>under</td></tr>
<tr><td>upon</td><td>school</td></tr>
<tr><td>green</td><td>clothes</td></tr>
<tr><td>horses</td><td>Lettuces</td></tr>
<tr><td>teapots</td><td>expensive</td></tr>
<tr><td>yummiest</td><td></td></tr>
</table>

Welcome to Spy School: Task 6

Hiding things is what we do best at MI5. But for you, as a trainee agent, it's important you know where those things are hidden. And also, that you know where to find them. So, here's a message for you. It's in the form of a rather untidy looking list:

difficult
library
remember
thought
purpose
occasion

But this is no ordinary list. It's just made to look that way. So, look at it again – very carefully. Don't read each word across the page. Instead, read down the letters a few times until, if your eyes are sharp, you'll spot a word spelled out in the middle of the piece. And that word is: *famous*.

You may know already that writing where the first letters of each line spell a word is an **acrostic**; and when the last letters of a piece form a word, this is a **telestich**. This form puts the word in the middle of a piece, and it's called a **mesostic**. *Mesos* was the ancient Greek word for 'middle'.

Here at MI5 we use lots of secret code-words and so we need lots of ways of hiding them in our messages. The code-words themselves are all stored safely on school spelling lists. *Famous* is on the Y3–4 list. Here's another mesostic for you, this time hiding a word on the Y5–6 list:

secretary
lightning
rhythm
stomach
foreign

That's right – *rhyme*. Each mesostic hides its code-word among words also on your spelling lists.

From your spelling list (see pages 143–144), choose one word you want as your secret code-word. Write it vertically down the middle of your page.

You are going to work one letter at a time down your word. Just look on your spelling sheet for words that use each of the letters of your code-word and write them across that word. Look especially for words where the letter you want is as near the middle as possible.

Messages must be accurate, so no spelling mistakes!

Welcome to Spy School: Task 7

Do you know what an agent does? And a travel agent? Of course you do! But what does a secret agent do? You don't know, and you're not meant to. Because it's secret. That's what spies do – keep secrets. Hide things, disguise things. The legendary agent, 007, James Bond, does this brilliantly with his many gadgets: the pen with its secret tracking device; the ring with a small camera built in; the key fob filled with just enough gas to stun an attacker.

Secrecy and disguise are vital in sending messages and so we need to hide them to keep them safe from prying eyes. And what better place to hide a message than in an innocent-looking nursery rhyme? Meant for the very young and already full of nonsense bits such as *Rub-a-dub-dub* and *Hey, diddle, diddle*, no-one would be suspicious. And so, that is precisely where we do bury keywords to send to our agents!

Here are two examples:

Diddle, diddle, dumpling, popular,	Mary, Mary, quite sincerely,
went to bed. Peculiar.	how does? Communicate?
Exercise, experiment.	With guarantee and cemetery
Diddle, diddle, dumpling, regular.	and pretty rhymes all in a row

As you may have spotted, each of those bits of nursery nonsense include five keywords on the Y3–4 and Y5–6 spelling lists (see pages 143–144). School spelling lists are another place nobody would expect MI5 to keep sensitive information!

First, choose your nursery rhyme – a short one or a single verse from a longer one. Now find the words that actually do rhyme at the line-ends of your nursery rhyme. Study your spelling list and find words that also rhyme (words that share the same-sounding last syllable). These are words which you can put into your rhyme to replace the original ones. You might be surprised at how many of the spelling list words rhyme, once you begin looking.

Don't worry at all about writing sensible English! Your task is to pass on keywords.

Only one thing matters in the words you choose: **syllables**. The number of syllables in each of your chosen list-words should be the same as the word or words you are replacing. For example, the three syllables of *popular* match the three syllables of the original, *my son John*. The four syllables of *communicate* match the four syllables of *your garden grow*. Count them to check.

Start your rewrite by writing the rhyme words as new line-endings. When these are in place, begin to fill in the rest of each line. Keep any words of the original rhyme you like but also look to see where you could replace them with more words from your spelling list. Aim to include 4–6 new words all together. You might also want to change the punctuation of the original to suit your rewrite.

   Cracking English Grammar in KS2 by David Horner

Welcome to Spy School: Task 8

Take a look at these words:

brunch	motel	cockapoo	banoffee	Bollywood	ginormous

Each of them is a **portmanteau word**. You say it port-man-toe and it simply means one word made by putting two words together. Or rather, smashing them together, so that only bits of the original words survive! For example:

Breakfast smashed into *lunch* makes <u>*brunch*</u>; *gigantic* smashed into *enormous* makes <u>*ginormous*</u>. Can you work out the others for yourself?

There are hundreds of portmanteau words in English. Some are old like *shepherd* from *sheep* and *herd* and some much newer, like *chillax* from *chill* and *relax*.

So, welcome now to Spy School's Great Word Smash! Here at MI5, we use school spelling lists to create our new portmanteau words. We use these to get important keywords to our agents. Here are some recently made examples with their new meanings:

ordiprise from *ordinary* and *surprise*: a treat that was meant to be exciting but wasn't.
diffiquest from *difficult* and *quest*: a tough challenge or a very hard task.
vegeraunt from *vegetable* and *restaurant*: a vegetarian restaurant.
mischindividual from *mischievous* and *individual*: someone very naughty.

Look through your spelling list and choose two words that you feel could be smashed together to make a brand-new portmanteau.

Experiment with different spellings of your new word before choosing the one you like best.

This new word needs now to go into a sentence or two to look like part of an ordinary message. So now, create a sentence, making it clear what the word means. For example:

> My birthday picnic was a real ordiprise. It rained the whole time.

> That mischindividual Robbie got himself in serious trouble last Thursday.

Who knows, one of your portmanteau words might one day become a dictionary item!

A key skill for any secret agent is the ability to crack and create codes. You will need to be able to make sense of coded messages – that look like gibberish to the untrained eye. You must also be able to write and send important messages in different codes, spelling out keywords correctly.

Your training in code work begins now. A code we use here at MI5 HQ will be explained to you. You will see below some single words. You will be given three tasks to carry out. As always, we are using words safely hidden away on school spelling lists.

Code 1: Forwards
Explanation: In Forwards code you encode each word using the next letter in the alphabet. For example, **SCHOOL** becomes **TDIPPM**. To crack words spelled in Forwards, then just come back to the letter before each one in the code. So, for example, **IPMJEBZ** becomes **HOLIDAY**.

Here are your three tasks, using words on the Y3–4 list:

Task 1: Here are three words in English for you to encode in Forwards:

    GUARD   **ISLAND**   **POTATOES**

Task 2: Here are three words in Forwards, but what are they in English?

    BEESFTT   **TFQBSBUF**   **XPNFO**

Task 3: Can you make a message of your own in Forwards, using any three nouns on your spelling list?

Code 2: Backwards
Explanation: In Backwards code you encode each word using the previous letter in the alphabet. So, for example, APPLE becomes ZOOKD. To crack words spelled in Backwards, just go on to the next letter in the alphabet. For example, BQTLAKD becomes CRUMBLE.

Here are three tasks for you, using words on the Y5–6 list:

Task 1: Here are three words in English for you to encode in Backwards:

    CATEGORY   **MARVELLOUS**   **SYSTEM**

Task 2: Here are three words in Backwards, but what are they in English?

    BZSDFNQX   **LZQUDKKNTR**   **RXRSDL**

Task 3: Can you make a message of your own in Backwards, using two adjectives and one noun from your spelling list?

Welcome to Spy School: Task 10

A key skill for any secret agent is the ability to crack and create codes. You will need to be able to make sense of coded messages – that look like gibberish to the untrained eye. You must also be able to write and send important messages in different codes, spelling out key words correctly.

Your training in code work begins now. A code we use here at MI5 HQ will be explained to you. You will see below some single words. You will be given three tasks to carry out. As always, we are using words safely hidden away on school spelling lists.

Code 1: Z to A
Explanation: In this code the alphabet is set out, not from A to Z but from Z to A. For example, **THUNDER** becomes **GSFMWVI**. And **HGLIN** decodes as **STORM**. If it helps, write out the alphabet and then underneath, write it again with the letters in reverse order.

Here are your three tasks, using words on the Y3–4 list:

Task 1: Here are three words in English for you to encode in Z to A:

ALTHOUGH   **MINUTE**   **DECIDE**

Task 2: Here are three words in Z to A, but what are they in English?

VCGIVNV   **RMXIVZHV**   **DVRTSG**

Can you make a message of your own in Z to A, using any three verbs on your spelling list?

Code 2: Half & Half
Explanation: Our alphabet has 26 letters. In this code, the first 13 letters (A to M) are written above the second half (N to Z). This code uses the letters above or below the actual English spelling. For example, **SPACE** becomes **FCNPR**. And **EBPXRG** decodes as **ROCKET**. If it helps, write out the alphabet, with the first half above the second half.

Here are three tasks for you, using words on the Y5–6 list:

Task 1: Here are three words in English for you to encode in Half & Half:

SHOULDER   **EXISTENCE**   **PREJUDICE**

Task 2: Here are three words in Half & Half, but what are they in English?

TBIREAZRAG   **RFCRPVNYYL**   **UNENFF**

Task 3: Can you make a message of your own in Half & Half, using one adverb, one adjective and one noun from your spelling list?

Welcome to Spy School: Task 11

A key skill for any secret agent is the ability to crack and create codes. You will need to be able to make sense of coded messages – that look like gibberish to the untrained eye. You must also be able to write and send correctly coded messages using different codes.

Your training in code work begins now. A code we use here at MI5 HQ will be explained to you. You will see below some single words. You will be given three tasks to carry out. As always, we are using words safely hidden away on school spelling lists.

Code 1: Numbers
Explanation: In this code you encode each word using the numbers 1 to 26 to stand for each letter as it appears in the alphabet. For example, **SECRET** becomes **19, 5, 3, 18, 5, 20**. To crack words spelled in Numbers, just change each number back to its matching letter. So, for example, **13, 5, 19, 19, 1, 7, 5** becomes **MESSAGE**.

Here are your three tasks using words on the Y3–4 list:

Task 1: Here are three words in English for you to encode in Numbers:

ENOUGH   **NATURAL**   **GROUP**

Task 2: Here are three words in Numbers, but what are they in English?

19, 20, 18, 1, 9, 7, 8, 20   **3, 9, 18, 3, 12, 5**   **16, 15, 19, 19, 9, 2, 12, 5**

Task 3: Can you make a message of your own in Numbers, using any three verbs on your spelling list?

Code 2: Roman
Explanation: In this code you encode each word using Roman numerals to replace the letters in the alphabet. For example, **ROMAN** becomes **XVIII, XV, XIII, I, XIV**. To crack words spelled in Roman, just change each Roman numeral back to its matching letter. For example, **XIV, XXI, XIII, V, XVIII, I, XII** becomes **NUMERAL**.

Here are your three tasks using words on the Y5–6 list:

Task 1: Here are three words in English for you to encode in **Roman**:

INTERRUPT   **VEHICLE**   **COMPETITION**

Task 2: Here are three words in Roman, but what are they in English?

XIX, XXV, XIII, II, XV, XII   **I, XIV, III, IX, V, XIV, XX**   **XIII, XXI, XIX, III, XII, V**

Task 3: Can you make a message of your own in Roman, using one verb, one adjective and one noun from your spelling list?

           Cracking English Grammar in KS2 by David Horner

Welcome to Spy School: Task 12

As you may know, MI5 hides many of its top-secret keywords on school spelling lists. We are always on the look-out for new ways of disguising our messages. Here is an example, using a children's word game. It is called **kinyume**. That's a word in the Swahili language and it means 'opposite' in English. Swahili is mainly spoken in East African countries such as Kenya and Tanzania.

Kinyume is all about syllables. A syllable is one sound in a word. So, jam (1), honey (2), marmalade (3). You count the beats in a word and that's the number of syllables.

To speak in Kinyume, children swap the order of the first and last syllables of words round. In a two-syllable word, first and last syllables swap places. So, *water* becomes *terwa*. In words of three or more syllables, the first and last syllables swap places and the rest of the word stays the same. So, *lemonade* becomes *adeonlem*. In one-syllable words, the first and last letters (or letter-sounds such as *th, sh, dge*) get swapped around. So, milk becomes *kilm*.

This seems an excellent way of disguising our spelling list words. Here are examples, first from the Y3–4 list:

> 1 syllable: *build > ildbu*
> 2 syllables: *answer > werans*
> 3 syllables: *calendar > darencal*

And these from the Y5–6 list:

> 1 syllable: *twelfth > ftheltw*
> 2 syllables: *occur > urocc*
> 3 syllables: *develop > opvelde*

Practise the game first by finding three words on your spelling list of 1, 2 and 3 syllables and swapping their first and last syllables (or letters/letter sounds) round.

You might find it helpful at first to write each syllable separately and link each one with a hyphen. So, *darencal* (calendar) becomes *dar-en-cal* and *opvelde* (develop) becomes *op-vel-de*.

Now choose any three fresh words from your spelling list and use them to make a one-sentence secret message. Add bits to your words if you need to and put in any new words you need for your sentence. Write your sentence in plain English first, checking it's correct and then translate it into Kinyume.

When you have made your sentence, practise saying it out loud. With a partner, you might go on to have whole (secret) conversations in Kinyume!

Doog kucl ingmak rouy cestensen ni Meyukin, oneeryev!

<table>
<tr><td></td><td></td><td></td><td></td></tr>
<tr><td></td><td></td><td></td><td></td></tr>
<tr><td></td><td></td><td></td><td></td></tr>
<tr><td></td><td></td><td></td><td></td></tr>
<tr><td></td><td></td><td></td><td></td></tr>
</table>

Cracking English Grammar in KS2 by David Horner

Appendix 1 Spelling

Notes and guidance (non-statutory)
Teachers should continue to emphasise to pupils the relationships between sounds and letters, even when the relationships are unusual. Once root words are learnt in this way, longer words can be spelt correctly, if the rules and guidance for adding prefixes and suffixes are also known.

National Curriculum Spelling Words Years 3–4

accident(ally)
actual(ly)
address
answer
appear
arrive

believe
bicycle
breath
breathe
build
busy/business

calendar
caught
centre
century
certain
circle
complete
consider
continue

decide
describe
different
difficult
disappear

early
earth
eight/eighth
enough
exercise
experience
experiment
extreme

famous
favourite
February
forward(s)
fruit

grammar
group
guard
guide

heard
heart
height
history

imagine
increase
important
interest
island

knowledge

learn
length
library

material
medicine
mention
minute

natural
naughty
notice

occasion(ally)
often
opposite
ordinary

particular
peculiar
perhaps
popular
position
possess(ion)
possible
potatoes
pressure
probably
promise
purpose

quarter
question

recent
regular
reign
remember

sentence
separate
special
straight
strange
strength
suppose
surprise

therefore
though/although
thought
through

various

weight
woman/women

National Curriculum Spelling Words Years 5–6

accommodate
accompany
according
achieve
aggressive
amateur
ancient
apparent
appreciate
attached
available
average
awkward

bargain
bruise

category
cemetery
committee
communicate
community
competition
conscience
conscious
controversy
convenience
correspond
criticise (critic + ise)
curiosity

definite
desperate
determined
develop
dictionary
disastrous

embarrass
environment
equip (–ped, –ment)
especially
exaggerate
excellent
existence
explanation

familiar
foreign
forty
frequently

government
guarantee

harass
hindrance

identity
immediate(ly)
individual
interfere
interrupt

language
leisure
lightning

marvellous
mischievous
muscle

necessary
neighbour
nuisance

occupy
occur
opportunity

parliament
persuade
physical
prejudice
privilege
profession
programme
pronunciation

queue

recognise
recommend
relevant
restaurant
rhyme
rhythm

sacrifice
secretary
shoulder
signature
sincere(ly)
soldier
stomach
sufficient
suggest
symbol
system

temperature
thorough
twelfth

variety
vegetable
vehicle

yacht

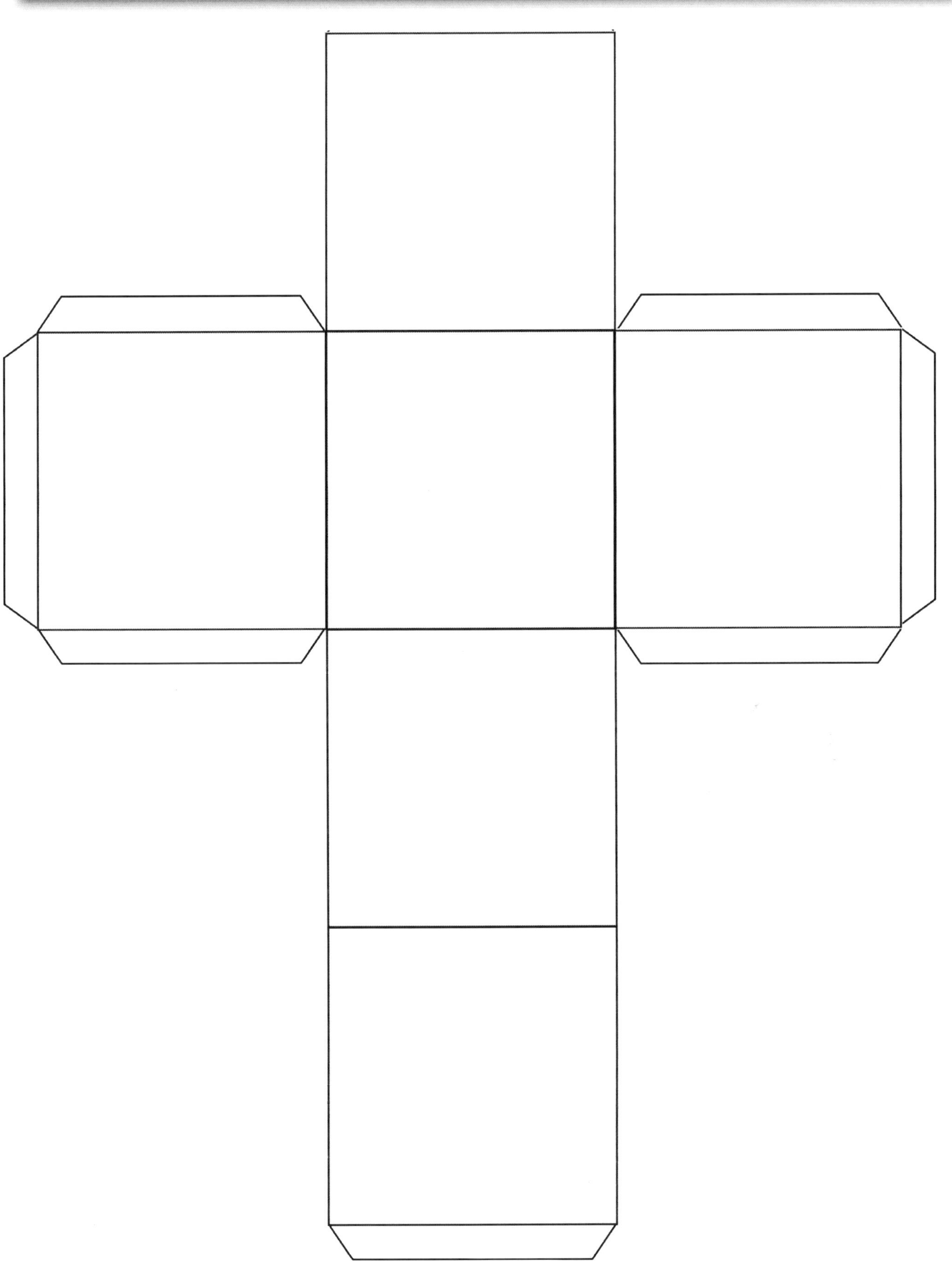

Index of Poetic Forms

Index of Grammatical Terms and Concepts

We are grateful to the following for permission to reproduce copyright material:

The poem "Slowly" by James Reeves from Complete Poems for Children, Faber & Faber, 2014. Reproduced by permission of David Higham Associates; The poem "Solo with Chorus" by Rose Fyleman, first published in Runabout Rhymes, 1941. Reproduced by permission of The Society of Authors as the Literary Representative of the Estate of Rose Fyleman; 2 lines from the poem "There was an old woman" by Charles Causley by Collected Poems for Children by Charles Causley, MacMillan, 1996. Reproduced by permission of David Higham Associates; and the poem "All The Ones They Call Lowly" by David Campbell. Reproduced by arrangement with the Licensor, The Estate of David Campbell c/o Curtis Brown (Aust) Pty Ltd.

References

Anonymous (1744) Tommy Thumb's Pretty Song Book. You can find lots of extra couplets for 'Oranges and Lemons' at www.wikipedia.org

Blake, Quentin (1996) A Puffin Book of Nonsense Verse, Puffin

Keats, John There was a Naughty Boy. Full four verse text at www.poetrybyheart.org.uk

Milne, A.A. (2020) The World of Winnie the Pooh, Egmont

Opie, Iona and Peter (eds.) (1992) I Saw Esau – The Schoolchild's Pocket Book, Walker Books

Schwartz, Alvin (1982) The Cat's Elbow, Farrar, Strauss, Giroux – a Sunburst Book

Shakespeare, William All plays available to download from www.shakespeare-online.com

Wells, Carolyn (1902) A Nonsense Anthology, Charles Scribner's Sons

Wordsworth, William I Wandered Lonely as a Cloud by William Wordsworth. Full text at www.poetryfoundation.org

Wright, Kit (1981) Hot Dog and Other Poems, Puffin

Photographic and Illustrative Credits

p.8/ 9	Very Short Stories (1)	Snowball fight Dentist chair	Michal Jarmaluk	Brilliant Publications Ltd Pixabay
p.10/ 11	Very Short Stories (2)	Welcome to Mars Zwei Teenager auf einem Kamel	Carol Jonas Grafikplusfoto	Brilliant Publications Ltd Fotolia.com
p13/ 14	The Ox and the Snaik	(Ox) Animals (Snake) Animal Crocodile	Urtica Design Open Clipart Vector Images Dmitry Abranov	Pixabay Pixabay Pixabay
p.15	A Spell to Make a Rainbow	Rainbow	Meneya	Pixabay
p.20	There's No Such Word as Spelling	Marshmallow	Leon Contreras	Unsplash
p.23	Two into One	Bat (Cricket) Bat Spring (Spring) Cherry blossom Jam Traffic jam	James Wainscoat CFPhotosin Photograghy James Allen Nagy Arnold Parej Richard Shilin Wang	Unsplash Unsplash Unsplash Unsplash Unsplash Pixabay
p.24	1 + 1 = 1	Shivering Lightning Funny face		Brilliant Publications Ltd Brilliant Publications Ltd Brilliant Publications Ltd
p.26/ 27	A Day in the Life of a Cloud	Cloud Ship	Brian Sarubbi Noupload	Pixabay Pixabay
p.35	Now You See It!	Mallard	Alexus Fotos	Pixabay
p.38	Super-Cinquains	Hedgehog Tunnel	MJ Jin Analogicus	Pixabay Pixabay
p.43	How to be Rude Like William Shakespeare	Thou art a boil…	Frank Endersby	Brilliant Publications Ltd
p.45	Lights, Camera, Action!	Jelly Baby	Jamie Street	Unsplash
p.47	Small is Beautiful	Ant Elephant	Clkr Free Vector Images Andremsantana	Pixabay Pixabay
p.50	A Parcel of Punctuation	Flock Keyring (Football Fan) Man	Gordon Johnson Open Clipart Vectors Damon Nofar	Pixabay Pixabay Pixabay
p.61	Ring Out, Wild Bells	Fruit Bells	Sundine Momental	Pixabay Pixabay
p.63/ 64	A Song About Myself	Hiking Girl	Free Photos AvroraDi	Pixabay Pixabay
p.65	All Change!	(Peacock) Animal	Lars Nissen	Pixabay
p.70	Solo with Chorus	People in Street	jonny-gios-6rMINFr-ogY	Unsplash
p.72	Dinosaur Discovery	Creativity	CDD20	Pixabay
p.75	First Words	Clydesdale	Jmrockeman	Pixabay

     Cracking English Grammar in KS2 by David Horner

p.78	Foxy Finishings	Fingers crossed Cat Power station Nuclear Explosion	Peter Timmerhues Dimitris Petsika JW Vein Gerd Altmann	Pixabay Pixabay Pixabay Pixabay
p.82	Joined-up Writing	Gingerbread Man	Molly Sage	Brilliant Publications Ltd
p.92/93	Sssssshhhhh – Letters Sleeping	Boys playing guitar watch silent T fisherman	Frank Endersby Clker-free Vector Images creozavr	Brilliant Publications Ltd Pixabay Brilliant Publications Ltd Pixabay
p.94	Police Report	One fine day…	Frank Endersby	Brilliant Publications Ltd
p.97	Definitely NOT the Bee's Knees!	Toast	Seriously low carb	Unsplah
p.110	Tall Tales	Giraffe/Moon (altered)	Lothar Dieterich	Pixabay
p.115	Talking to the Animals	Garter snake Grass hopper Frog Worm	Nikki W Journey Anrita 1705 Suju-photo Patricia Main Degrave	Pixabay Pixabay Pixabay Pixabay
p.119/120	Witches' Brew	Three witches (Macbeth) Witch and cauldron	Ray and Corrine Burrows Molly Sage	Brilliant Publications Ltd Brilliant Publications Ltd
p.121	Writing Painting	Pub closed	Frank Endersby	Brilliant Publications Ltd